I0087477

Blogging My Way to Indie Success: Blogs, Articles, and Writing Advice

by L.J. Sellers
Author of the bestselling Detective Jackson
series and standalone thrillers

Cover art by Gwen Thomsen Rhoads

ISBN: 9780983213888
Published in the USA by Spellbinder Press

Table of Contents

Dear Reader

Thank you for purchasing this collection of personal essays, blogs, writing advice, and nonfiction features. Most of the selections were written between the time I published my first novel in October 2007 and my eighth one in August 2011. It's hard to believe it's only been four years. So much has happened. It was fun to go back and read some of my hopes, fears, and goals. I'm happy to report I accomplished nearly everything I set out to do.

I created this book in response to readers who've commented that they love my nonfiction writing—as well as my novels—and suggested I publish a collection of features. Many of the blogs I wrote ended with a question for readers, and I left a few in place, so feel free to locate the blog on my website and add your comment. I check for new comments every day.

I've organized the articles into categories as best I could, but you'll discover that many of the topics overlap. The first chapter includes published essays and blogs that offer personal information, with the idea that readers might like to know more about me, the person behind the novels. I've also included a long chapter with writing and editing advice. The final chapter is a collection of profiles I wrote for our local paper, *The Register-Guard*, during the year I worked there. They feature amazing people in my hometown of Eugene.

Typically, I listed the blogs in the order I wrote them, with the date included to give context to material that may seem dated already. The Writing and Editing Advice chapter, on the other hand, I tried to organize logically.

This selection only represents about half of the blogs I penned during that timeframe and only a quarter of the newspaper articles. I also wrote five novels in that period. As my husband says, I'm a "woman of many words."

I hope that continues to be true, and I hope you enjoy the material.

—L.J.

Chapter 1: Personal Essays

Trikes, Tattoos, and Turing 40
(Published in *The Register-Guard*, 2/98)

Last Friday my husband turned 40. This weekend he's putting the finishing touches on a three-wheeled motorcycle he built from scratch during the last few months. Are these things related? I think so. First, the man is no mechanic. A fine cabinetmaker and all-around handyman, yes. But typically, I can't even get him to change the oil in my car without weeks of nagging. So last fall when he announced he was going to build a vehicle, I was stunned. And skeptical. I kept it to myself of course, after gently asking, "Are you sure that's what you want to do, honey? You know how much you hate to work on cars."

But the *trike* was different—a funky blend of Volkswagen bug and Goldwing motorcycle that resembles a mutant dune buggy with fat tires and cool handle bars. The trike became an obsession.

First he brought home the decrepit orange *bug* that would become a fixture in our yard for months. Then he spent hours searching the internet for information, downloading hundreds of trike pictures in the process. Entire weekends were consumed with trips to Harrisburg and Springfield, tracking down obscure parts and make-shift pieces. Then the long haul began, night after night spent in the garage, step by painful step, putting the thing together.

My husband is not an electrician either, but he mastered the wiring system of a VW and recreated it to make the trike street legal. He also taught himself to weld steel, do extensive bodywork, apply fiberglass, and paint metal. It's been a tremendous amount of work. I've never seen him so happy. Or so obsessed.

Turning 40 isn't easy. You hear about men buying spendy red sports cars or running off with their secretaries. I'm proud of him for turning his mid-life anxiety into a creative endeavor that the whole family can enjoy.

But I'm glad it's over. The weekly trips to Furrow's and Knecht's began to drain our checking account. And I started to think he'd conceived the project just as an excuse to accumulate every tool he ever wanted. (Who really needs a compression gage?) The constant dust and stink of Bondo got old after a while too. But I'm mostly anxious to get out on the road. I grew up with motorcycles and have missed the rush of adrenaline that kicks in as you swing your leg over the seat and fire up the motor.

I'll be 40 soon enough myself, so I know what he's been feeling. In fact, I found myself in a tattoo parlor yesterday afternoon having a blue butterfly etched into my calf. *How did this happen?* my mother and husband both wanted to know.

It was easier than you might think.

The night before, a youngster where I work announced her intention of getting a tattoo, and I was hit with a pang of jealously. I'd wanted one since I was a teenager. But I'd always worried that someday I'd be 40 and cringe at the sight, hearing that nag in my head say, *What the hell were you thinking?*

But that day was almost here, and so still was the desire. Even the design and color I wanted remained unchanged after 20 years. When another co-worker, also approaching the big 4-0, echoed my feelings, I thought, *why not?*

It was a great adventure, a day filled with the same nervous excitement I experience before boarding an airplane—that tumultuous feeling of knowing that when I walked out of there, I would never be exactly the same again. And liking the thought.

Yes, I know, someday I'll be 60, and possibly I'll look at my tattoo and shake my head. But I'll know what I was thinking when I got it.

I was thinking that life is short and the thrills are few and far between once mid-life, parentally-inspired maturity sets in. So to hell with convention. Next weekend I'll throw my tattooed leg over the seat of a trike and ride with the wind.

Current note from the author: My husband is now a full-time trike builder. Check out his work at http://hutchisontrikes.com

An Unlikely Warrior
(Published in *The Register-Guard*, 5/98)

The game stayed with me. Even after the paint washed off and the stinging subsided, I couldn't stop thinking about getting back in there, playing better, staying lower and moving around more. What I really wanted was to score, just once to hear someone yell, "I'm hit" after I pumped off a round. Now I have to go back. And that wasn't the plan.

I'm talking about paintballing, of course. Old news to everyone under twenty-five, but quite an adventure for this thirty-eight year-old writer. My sons had all tried it on different occasions. Two didn't care to go back, but the third got hooked. He spent his hard-earned paper route money at fifteen dollars a session without hesitation.

Then he started in on me. "You gotta go with me, Mom, you'll love it." I had mixed feelings so I put him off. But he is tenacious—as only a thirteen-year-old can be— and he wore me down. One evening after I'd painted the dining room he looked at me and said, "You're already covered with paint, let's go now." It was the last thing I felt like doing, but being a practical person, I decided it was a good time to get it over with.

When we walked into Hotshots, one of the kids looked at my paint-splattered clothes and said, "Cool, you play a lot." That made me smile. Until I read the consent form, which had a little disclaimer about the possibility of "dismemberment or death."

My hands trembled as I pulled on the bright pink mask. Looking around at the other players, a small group of boys aged thirteen to fifteen, I told myself, *It's only paint and they're only kids.* But the minute I stepped into that dark room with sawdust floors and scattered barricades, it was real. My heart pounded with the thought of snipers, armed with assault weapons stealthily moving in to shoot me on sight. The first "bullet" that zinged by my head made my heart leap into my throat. After the initial impulse to take cover, I found an opening in the barricade, stuck my gun through and returned fire. The satisfying smack of a paintball slamming into wood, excited me. I was suddenly gripped with a desire to get them before they could get me.

My son knows me well.

After a few minutes I was sucking wind and vibrating with adrenaline. And I run six miles a day. Fortunately, the game is played in short sessions with players going out as they are hit until only one person or team remains in the arena. My first hit was in the neck, "the worst" the kids claimed as they clamored around me offering sympathetic comments. But I was stoic. Not a whimper. Yes, it hurt, but not for long and not enough to discourage me from going back in.

I was hit quickly again in the second game, then learned to stay lower to the ground and be more aggressive. The fourth game was the best. It came down to me and a fourteen-year-old named Ryan who was very good. When I realized it was just the two of us, I had this wild surge of confidence, this overwhelming need to nail him with a paintball. I went after the kid with suicidal aggression, running, ducking, dodging, and pumping off rounds as fast as I could. He responded with his own offensive and we got into a close-range shoot-out that was so intense it made me hyperventilate. When he finally nailed me in the leg—as I threw myself behind a barricade—I laughed out loud with relief.

To say I got into it is an understatement. Between games the kids would be in the foyer, talking about their hits, no hurry to start a new game. But with each round

I was more anxious to get back in there. Near the end of our prepaid hour, I started to sound like a drill sergeant, "Let's go, let's go."

After an hour I was soaked with sweat, hoarse from sucking up oxygen, and almost giddy with fatigue and adrenaline overload. But I never took anyone out with a paintball, or at least none of the kids would claim a hit from me. And it eats at me still. If only I'd done this or tried that. If only I'd had more time.

Now I have to go back. And that wasn't the plan.

Career Misfits
(Published in *The Register-Guard*, 3/99)

It's come to my attention lately that a growing number of people seem to be particularly unqualified—at least on the surface—for the job they do. I can't help but wonder how they survive in their chosen profession.

For example, a woman I met recently proudly claimed to be a hairdresser. I glanced at her *coiffure*—a white-blond crewcut with dark roots—and thought to myself, *Never in a million years would I let this woman touch my hair. I could achieve more sympathetic results with chemotherapy.* The poor woman might be surprisingly good with a pair of scissors, but who in their right mind would take the chance?

Or what about the guy I waited on who had trouble figuring a 15 percent gratuity and asked for my help. I'm no math whiz, but if someone wants to leave a nice tip, I can round off the total and figure it my head in three seconds flat. I was mildly surprised when he complimented my arithmetic skills. A moment later when he announced that he taught middle school math, I bruised my lips holding back an astonished sputter. Who hired this man? Could he even pass one of his own quizzes? No wonder our kid's math scores are slipping.

If I hadn't been there, I wouldn't believe it myself.

Then there's the woman I encounter socially, very sweet, but substantially overweight. One evening I asked what she did for a living. Are you cringing? Of course, she owns a weight-loss clinic. I stood there nodding, completely speechless for the first time in my life. What should I have said? "New in the business?"

Seriously, how can you sell a product when you're visible proof of its failure? It would be like George Costanza trying to pitch Rogaine. Don't they know better? Doesn't it hurt? Or is it possible they simply lack a sense of irony? If there were only a few of these characters, I'd call it a karmic snafu and let it go. But these people are everywhere!

There's the guy behind the counter at the health-food store who raves about the benefits of nutritional supplements yet looks like he hasn't eaten or slept well in weeks. The mechanic who lives next door and needs a ride to work once a week because his car won't start. And the friend who struggles to make a living as a remodeler, while his own home is such a cosmetic nightmare I'd love to torch it and make him start from scratch.

Does anybody ever say anything to these misfits? Let them know—subtly of course—that they might be in the wrong business? I'm fairly outspoken (people who know me might question the accuracy of the word *fairly*), but I've never suggested a career change to anyone who seemed happy in their job.

I once worked with a cook who loved to grow exotic plants. When he told me he was studying psychology at the university, I impulsively blurted out, "Why? If you love plants, study botany. The key to happiness in life is finding something you love to do, then doing it until you're good enough to make a living."

I stand by my words. If these mismatched folks love what they do and are happy doing it, then more power to them. I will continue to bite my tongue—and ask for references.

Blogs
My Other Names (8/08)

It's serendipitous that Dani tagged me in this meme. I was just thinking about why I have always used my initials as a writer, as opposed to my given name: Linda. When I was young, I heard my father say that men were better writers than women. So from my first day as a journalist, I submitted my work under the name L.J., so readers could not prejudge my writing based on gender.

And as an employee in the work place, there were usually too many other Lindas, so I always said, "Call me L.J." But if I were to write under pseudonyms, here are some possibilities.

1. Real name plus my husband's last name: **Linda Hutchison**

2. Gangsta name: (first 3 letters of real name plus izzle) **Linizzle**

3. Detective name: (favorite color/favorite animal) **Blue Lemur**

4. Soap opera/porn name: (middle name and street) **Jean Lorrane**

5. Star Wars name: (first 3 letters last name, first 2 letters first name) **Selli**

6. Superhero name: (second favorite color/favorite drink) **Fuchsia Pepper**

7. Witness Protection name: (parents' middle names) **Patricia Clark**

8. Goth name: (black plus the name of one of your pets) **Black Magoo**

My Greatest Fan (8/08)

I'd like to introduce you to Sergeant Isaac Hutchison, my greatest fan. He's a military police officer stationed in El Paso, Texas. He just found out he's going back to Iraq in January. He already spent a year and half of his young life there, but he serves his country willingly and proudly. And I am proud—beyond words—of him.

My proudest moment as an author came many years ago after a midnight phone call. I stumbled to the phone, half asleep, half panicked, thinking, *What's wrong?* Isaac's voice came on the phone and said, "Oh my God. You blew me away." I still didn't know what he was talking about. He went on, "I just finished your novel, and I had to call you and tell you how much I loved it. I loved your characters. I want to be Eric."

He recently told me he read that particular novel, *The Baby Thief*, four times. And it's possible my story character shaped who he turned out to be—a thoughtful, passionate man who cares about so much of the world beyond himself.

Isaac was also my first fan. He started reading my novels almost 20 years ago when they were still in manuscript form. Any time I printed a copy of a novel or first three chapters that wasn't good enough to send out, the stack of paper would go into a recycling box for the kids to use as scratch paper for math or drawings. Isaac would grab a stack of paper from the box, take it to his room, and read chunks of my stories. They were often just bits and pieces, 10 pages of this section and 40 pages of something else. He would often ask me to tell him how it all turned out.

Years later, he was as excited as I was to finally see my novels in print. Today, he brags about me and my writing to anyone who will listen. Now he's waiting anxiously for the next installment. Whenever I'm having anxiety about not being good enough, I can count on him for moral support. I'm lucky to have such a fan. And such a fine son.

10 Things to Know About Me (8/08)

Lesa said I could use this opportunity to introduce myself, and who can resist that invitation? If you're familiar with my current novel, *The Sex Club*, you know three things about me already:

1. I'm not shy.

2. I'm not afraid to take chances.

3. I write from the heart about things that are important to me.

I'm one of those lucky people who knew from a young age what I wanted to be when I grew up. I envisioned myself as a broadcast journalist, living the single life in New York and covering all the big events. Instead, I ended up in Eugene, Oregon, working for a pharmaceutical magazine and writing novels in my spare time while raising three boys...and various other children. I know more about prescription drugs than I ever thought I would. I ended up with more children than I had planned, and it's taken a lot longer to get my novels to the public than I ever imagined.

I could tell you about my two-decade struggle to get published, a story that involves several novels, several agents, and several close calls. But other authors have taken similar paths, so instead I'll tell you some things that are specific to me and my writing:

4. I took a comedy writing class, so I could improve my comedy scripts, and had to perform my material as a final grade. It was such good fun (and I was surprisingly good), so I wrote more material and went back to perform several more times. Yet, public speaking terrifies me. And my crime novels are not humorous.

5. I write the kind of novels I like to read: fast-paced crime stories that combine mystery and suspense with realistic engaging characters.

6. I write about antagonists who are in most ways ordinary people with a deep character flaw, who commit crimes out of fear, frustration, self-protection, or misguided passion.

I'm currently writing a series featuring Detective Wade Jackson. The series is set in Eugene, and Jackson is a veteran detective raising a 14-year-old daughter. He purposefully is NOT a hard-drinking, violence-prone cynic loner. He's a likable man who's dedicated to his job and his daughter and tries to balance the two. The first novel in the series, *The Sex Club*, has garnered dozens of rave reviews. It gives me such joy to finally have a novel out there that people are reading and enjoying. Please don't be put off by the title. The story isn't X-rated. I debated at length about whether to use that provocative title, but so far no one has come up with anything more fitting.

Recently, I completed a second novel featuring Detective Jackson. It's called *Secrets to Die For*, and I'm optimistic that I'll have a publishing date soon. I also have a standalone thriller, *The Baby Thief*, which I hope to see published some day as well. And I have a collection of *practice* novels gathering cyber dust on my hard drive.

Here are a few unusual facts about me:

7. I once rode my bicycle from Oregon to the Grand Canyon, including up and over Donner Pass, elevation 10,000 feet.

8. I have spent my whole life in search of a comfortable, attractive pair of shoes and once wrote a comedy screenplay called *Shoes*. (It placed third in a competition.)

And here are a few business-like facts:

9. Most days, I work from six in the morning until about ten at night, but a lot of what I do is so enjoyable that I don't think of it as work. That is the joy of being a writer.

10. I am also a freelance editor. I split my editing time between corporate reports/academic books and fiction manuscripts. After writing fiction, editing fiction is my next favorite thing.

Author's current update: I'm a full-time novelist and no longer edit fiction.

The Secret to Happiness (8/08)

Lately, strategies for happiness have been in the news. Two prominent ideas have a common theme. The first is to stop complaining. Completely. No exceptions. You train yourself to do this by wearing a band on your wrist. Every time you complain, you have to move it to the other wrist. The goal is to go 21 days without complaining—or moving the band. I've never made it 21 days (because some whining is cathartic!), and I stopped wearing the band (it's summer!). But I keep doing the mental checks. It's very productive in controlling negative thought cycles.

A second secret to happiness, which has been promoted recently in articles by psychologists and counselors, is to be grateful every day. They say the strategy is most effective when you write down, every day, the things you are grateful for (more listmaking!). The theory is that feeling grateful is a clear path to happiness. And it works by keeping your thought processes in a positive mode.

If you throw in the concept from the popular self-help book, *The Secret*, the formula for happiness is this: Stop complaining, express gratitude every day, and ask the universe for what you want.

The universe has not yet given me everything I want, but I'm happy in my effort to go out and get it for myself.

12 Questions (8/08)

1) Computer, longhand, or other? The only thing I write with a pen are lists. I have loved computers for writing anything and everything since the first day I sat down at one.

2) Coffee or tea? Both! And lots of it. I start with strong black coffee (grinding the beans and all), then switch to green tea (lemongrass or jasmine), then drink licorice tea at night. (*Update: I no longer drink caffeine.* ☹)

3) Day or night? As my blog's subhead says, *First thing every morning.* I can, and do, write at night sometimes, but I struggle with it.

4) Favorite genre to write? I write what I love to read: mystery/suspense. I also write comedy for my standup routine and I have written three comedy screenplays. I love writing comedy, but it's very hard work. Some people manage to combine crime and comedy, but for me, they're like oil and water, and I just can't mix 'em…yet.

5) Pencil or pen to edit? I edit my own work on screen, then switch to paper for the final read. I also edit my clients' fiction on paper. I use three writing utensils: the purple pen mark means "make this edit," the pencil means "consider this syntax edit," and the yellow highlighter means "look at this repetition or inconsistency."

6) Unusual writing quirk or trait? I wish I had something funny or cute to tell you about. In truth, I write fiction very lean. My first drafts are mostly action and dialogue. Then I have to go back and fill in with more detail and characterization.

7) Writing from home or writing in a cozy café? I use an ergonomic keyboard, I can't function without a mouse, and my workstation at home lets me stand up and work for periods throughout the day. Why would I go anywhere else?

8) Music or silence while your write? Years ago, I could write with three boys playing Nintendo in the room. Now I like it quiet. But I'm going to try Karen's suggestion of playing certain music for certain scenes.

9) Favorite motivational writing quote? My own: Life is short. Get it done.

10) Favorite bookmark? I use one of my own for *The Sex Club*. It reminds me that I can write too.

11) Favorite fictional character of all time? Tough question. Who comes to mind today is Irwin Fletcher, made famous by Chevy Chase. I loved the books and the movies! He's a great example of combining crime and comedy.

12) Most admired living writer today? I can't pick a living writer because there are too many. My favorite writer of all time though is Lawrence Sanders. He's incredibly versatile and always entertaining.

In Case You're Not Sick of Me Yet (1/09)

Once you've been tagged, you are supposed to write a note with 16 random things, facts, habits, or goals about you. (P.S. I'm not big on rules, so I may not get to 16. Nor are you obligated to play if I tag you.)

1. I spent my early childhood in Las Vegas, then the rest in Cave Junction, Oregon. Had my family not moved to Podunk, I would probably be a stripper or showgirl instead of a writer.

2. I once rode my bicycle from Eugene to the Grand Canyon, crossing Donner Pass, an elevation of about 10,000 feet. Three straight days of uphill, heart-pumping fun.

3. Every birthday, I ride up a long steep hill just to prove to myself that I still can.

4. I am an addict . . . who no longer indulges in much of anything. I quit drinking December 17, 1989, and I quit smoking cigarettes January 1, 1991. New Year's resolutions can be effective.

5. My favorites foods are grilled ribeye steak and cold watermelon. If I had to choose two things to live on forever, they would make the cut.

6. I go bowling with my three brothers once a week. I never seem to get any better, but I don't care. It's fun and I love my brothers.

7. I graduated from the University of Oregon with a BA in journalism, then worked as a food server for years while my kids were young because of the flexible hours.

But I've been doing freelance writing and editing for 25 years.

8. I was born in July and love summer! The only time the world seems right to me is when the sky is blue and the air is warm.

9. It's hard to choose, but I think my life-long favorite author is Lawrence Sanders. He's so versatile—police procedurals, futuristic thrillers, and the lovable Archy McNally.

10. I took a vow at the beginning of 2008 to not buy any clothes, shoes, or purses for the entire year. I broke it only once in October to buy a business-casual jacket for Bouchercon, then didn't even wear it because the weather was so warm. (Doing my part to crash the economy!)

11. I'm always swearing off of something. (See #4) This year it's diet Dr. Pepper (love the stuff!). I never had a problem with drinking too much of it until they made caffeine-free diet Dr. Pepper, which I can drink right up until bedtime.

Life Changing Moments (6/09)

Milestones tend to make me reflective. Often they make me want to reassess and regroup. Not this one. Nearly 20 years ago, I sat down and started my first novel. I remember the scene clearly: a Commodore computer set up in the bedroom, a cup of coffee in hand, and a yellow reporter's tablet with some sketched-out ideas.

Much has happened in my writing career since then, and we'd need a whole pot of coffee to cover it. Two events, though, stand out as game-changers in how I lived my life. The first was an epiphany I had about nine years after starting that first novel. I read an interview with a scriptwriter who'd recently sold his first screenplay for big money. When the interviewer asked if he would do anything differently, given the chance, the writer said, "If I had known it would take ten years to sell a script, I would have found a better day job."

That hit home with me. At the time, I was waiting tables and doing a little freelance writing. There's not much editorial work in Eugene, OR, but still, working as a food server was making me feel bad about myself. Also, I had recently failed to sell a novel, even though my top-notch agent told me we had an offer. Crushing!

I realized I had to find a better day job—immediately! I had to resume my career and put my journalism degree and inquisitive mind to work in a productive and satisfying capacity. Hating your job is no way to live. How you spend every day is critical.

So I stopped living for the future—that day when my novels would sell and my life would change. I found a job as a magazine editor, and I accepted, on some level, that nonfiction writing and editing would be my career and that it would be enough.

It was great move. I instantly felt better about myself. Over time, I developed extensive editing and layout skills that would serve me well for a lifetime in publishing. (I also learned a lot about prescription drugs!) I kept writing fiction in my spare time though. It's an addictive little hobby.

Seven years later, the magazine moved to New York and I was laid off. While I looked for work, I used the opportunity to finish writing *The Sex Club*, the novel that would finally launch my career as a mystery-suspense author. Still needing the security of a paycheck, I soon found a position with an educational publisher. It was a wonderful job, but it took every bit of brain power I had. In the two and a half years with that company, I didn't write a single word of new fiction. In the long run, it was not a happy time in my life.

Then last March, as the economy tanked, they laid me off. It was nerve-racking but also incredibly liberating. I decided to do things a little differently this time. I decided to write first thing every morning, no matter what. (Thus the name of my blog: Write First, Clean Later.) I developed a freelance editing business that allowed me to work on my schedule—with the paid work done during afternoons, evenings, and weekends. Mornings were for writing novels.

I love my new life! My bathroom is perpetually messy, dinner is often an unimaginative freezer-to-oven meal, and there's laundry backed up everywhere. I'm also never sure if the next freelance gig will pay the bills. But since that lifestyle change fifteen months ago, I've written two more Detective Jackson novels, and I'm working on a fourth. One of those stories will be published in September, and another book will be released in August next year.

My husband says he's never seen me so happy. It's the first time in my life I've put my novel writing first. Making a living, raising kids, taking care of an extended family, and keeping the house together were always the priorities. Those things are all still important, I just don't let them get in the way anymore. I also realize how lucky I am to be in this position.

One of the best things about this new life is the social networking. I love blogging and sharing both writing and marketing advice with other novelists. I love meeting writers and readers online and getting to know them. I love attending conferences and being a part of the crime fiction community.

The takeaway message is this: Enjoy every day and every task. And make time to do what you love, whether it's writing, or skydiving, or quilting. It's the only way to be truly happy.

The Gift of 50 (7/09)

Today I am 50.

If you only knew how hard that was to say. I've struggled to get my brain around this number for weeks now. I thought for a while if I never actually said it out loud, no one would know, and I could maintain the illusion that I was still in my late forties, which sounds so much nicer. But that's crap. It's just a number. So to be true to my nature—the queen of too much information—I decided to go the other direction and make an actual announcement.

All the wonderful birthday wishes that have been pouring in from online friends and family have really helped. Thank you for those.

I keep thinking of my sister, Kerry, who died two months after turning 48. And my two sisters-in-law, Arlene and Rose, who died at 39 and 54. I have no right to lament this birthday. I am alive! And healthy! If that weren't enough, I'm also in a great place in my life right now.

So I've decided to embrace 50 for what it is—a gift. Going forward, I hope I have the good sense to express gratitude every day for this simple gift of life.

Healthcare and Job Choices (8/09)

A thoughtful letter to the editor this morning caught my attention. In essence, he said that many people stay in jobs that are unhealthy for them, physically and or emotionally, just to keep the healthcare benefits for their family. What a sad tradeoff.

I believe it happens more often than you think. My brother, for example, stayed in a job he hated for 20

27

years because his wife had diabetes and couldn't work and he felt trapped into providing healthcare benefits for her. Changing jobs was too risky. Many employers won't add a spouse or child with a pre-existing condition to the new employee's policy. So he stayed in a miserable work environment until he developed diabetes himself. How many thousands of people are making that unhealthy choice?

I'm currently facing a similar situation. A full-time writer/editor position just opened at the newspaper. It's the same position I applied for (with mixed feelings), then didn't get (to my relief) four months ago. After four stressful months, the woman who got the job was fired. Now they're asking me if I want it.

The truth is I don't want the job, I just want the healthcare benefits. But if I get the position and end up stressed, unhappy, and not focused on my novels, how can it be worth it? Since I was laid off early last year and ended up with two, flexible part-time jobs, I've been happier—and healthier—than ever before. So I'm starting to think that being happy is the best health tonic of all.

Wouldn't it be good for our entire culture if healthcare was easy to access and not linked to employment? And no one had to make a bad job choice based on fear of losing a loved one or going bankrupt from medical bills?

Crime Scene Crazy
(Published in *Mystery Scene* magazine 9/10)

Crime writers are a quirky bunch, me included. Our idea of fun is a little different. For example, I've been making calls and sending emails to the local medical examiner and pathologist, begging to be allowed to witness an autopsy. I've already interviewed the ME and took detailed notes as he described the sights and sounds of dissecting a dead human being. But no, that's not enough, I really need to see it for myself.

My detective character, Wade Jackson, attends the autopsy of every homicide victim he investigates, so I feel compelled to experience it first hand, at least once. The ME says rookie cops sometimes pass out the first time they hear the whine of the Stryker saw as it cuts through the ribcage, so I see the autopsy as a challenge. The pathologist finally consented, and I'm now waiting for the call, as excited as any game show contestant would be.

There's more.

The other day I had an interview scheduled with the sergeant who supervises the violent crimes unit here in Eugene, Oregon. We had planned to talk about a fictional homicide setting with multiple dead bodies and plenty of blood spatter. As I was driving down to see her, she called and said she had to cancel because they'd "had a homicide" and she was at the scene.

Heart pounding, I squealed, "Can I come down? Please." To my surprise and delight, she agreed. I made a wild U-turn and headed for the park, giddy with excitement. It was true *Castle* moment. I was headed to a real homicide!

After a few minutes, the sane, responsible part of my brain kicked in, and I felt guilty about my glee. A person was dead, I reminded myself. Tragically murdered. Have a little respect. I slapped myself to wipe the smile off my face.

My somber moment lasted all of ten seconds, then I was grinning again and searching my bag to see if I had my camera and calling my husband to share my excitement. Yes, all of that simultaneously, while driving.

I'm happy to report I arrived safely, but the actual crime scene was a huge disappointment. It was in a public park by the river, and the detectives had strung up crime scene tape around a one-acre area. The victim, a homeless man, was fifty yards away, behind a short, makeshift plastic wall. Apparently, sensitive locals have complained about the police leaving dead bodies laying in the open while they take pictures and collect trace evidence. So I didn't get anywhere near the corpse. Nor did I see a single drop of blood or sit in on an interrogation.

As for the detectives at the scene, they were standing around the hood of a car eating pizza! Such a let down.

It was just bad timing. I know from my many interviews with homicide detectives that they work round-the-clock for the first few days, and the scenes they process are often gruesome. I've looked at the pictures. I've picked their brains for details. What did the room smell like? Was the body bloated? How much blood was on the floor? Do dead bodies really make noises?

My curiosity for these details is limitless. I've spent hours with a crime scene technician discussing the dozens of dead bodies he's seen and hearing in detail what kind of insects would lay eggs in a corpse found in a wooded area within the city limits. For my next novel, *Passions of the Dead*, I grilled a SWAT sergeant while he described exactly how a sniper would kill a hostage taker.

I'm not a morbid person by nature. In fact, one of my pastimes is performing standup comedy, and I would rather dance than do just about anything else. But I am curious about nearly everything, and I like to get all the death details right for my police procedural novels.

I want my series to be realistic. The fact that it's set in a mid-size college town can be limiting. We have our share of murders, they're just not particularly exotic or complicated and the perpetrators tend to be rather stupid. When I plot my novels, I try to find the right balance between a story that is complex enough to engage readers and one that is believable for its physical and social setting.

We've had our share of missing women in Eugene, so in my latest book, *Thrilled to Death,* Jackson investigates the disappearance of two young women with nothing in common. When one turns up dead with no obvious wounds, the crime scene adds to the mystery, and the investigation grows more puzzling.

As for the scene I wrote involving multiple bodies and blood spatter, you'll have to wait for my fourth book, due out next year. In the meantime, I'll keep looking for gruesome opportunities to add to my resume. It's in the job description.

Why Crime Fiction Is Important (8/10)

Does the detective writer sit in the same chair at the table of literature as a transvestite cousin at a family gathering?

Say what? This question came to me, via Facebook, from a researcher working on a PhD dissertation about the mystery/crime genre. The analogy both amused and disheartened me. I've always known that genre fiction isn't considered to be in the same category as literary fiction, but I never let it bother me as a reader or novelist—until the moment I was compared to a transvestite cousin at a family gathering. Not that there's anything wrong with transvestites.

But back to my point. You've all read the articles in which the reviewer declares that a particular mystery or thriller "transcends the genre," as if crime fiction had built-in limits and readers had to approach it with low expectations. What a load of nonsense.

For me, crime novels offer some of the best reading on nearly every level. Crime fiction confronts the realities of life across various cultures more often and more honestly than mainstream, or literary, fiction does.

Crime novels are particularly suited to exploring provocative social issues and showing how those issues affect various people's lives, often from various characters' perspectives. Crime fiction can be surprisingly poignant and analytical about problems such as illegal immigration, human trafficking, and drug use. Other crime novels highlight deep-rooted cultural ills, such as racism, sexism, bigotry, and the dangers of stereotypes. Or they show a stereotype in all its glory, reminding us of why we have stereotypes and how we all fit into one ...just a little bit. Crime novels often force us to see the world from perspectives that surprise us and make us think outside our comfort zone.

Crime fiction gives us a medium through which we can vicariously win the struggles in our society between good and evil. As crime writers and readers, we get to make sense of things that would otherwise haunt us. We learn why the family across the street disappeared one day. Sometimes, it helps us sleep better and sometimes not, but at least we know one version of what happened.

We get to experience the triumph of good over evil. We get to be the good guy, the hero who rescues the kidnapped child or saves the president's life... for a few hours anyway. We get to drag the bad guys off to jail or shoot them dead if "they need killin'"—fantasies we can't act out in our everyday lives. The real-world events around us can be cruel and unjust and mysterious. It's important to our collective mental health to experience justice, order, and revelation through fiction.

Crime fiction also brings us to terms with the duality within ourselves. We're all deeply flawed, with the capacity for great goodness as well as for deceit, jealousy, schadenfreude, addiction, selfishness, and more. When crime fiction heroes—detectives, FBI agents, prosecutors—show such flaws, we not only relate to them, we forgive ourselves for the same transgressions. When a killer calls his mother or pets a stray dog, we hate him a little less and remember to look for good qualities in everyone.

Crime novels explore relationships as well as any other genre. What better way to test a bond between spouses, friends, or parent and child than becoming embroiled in a crime, either as victim, suspect, or perpetrator. Similar to natural disasters, the aftermath of a crime can bring out the bes, or worst, in humans.

The crime genre is also rich with possibilities for exploring the complexity of the human condition. Victims become predators; predators become victims. A person is guilty, but not in the way you've been led to believe.

Most of all, crime fiction is full of surprises. And readers love the unexpected. When was the last time a reviewer used the word *surprise* or *twist* or *unexpected* when discussing a literary novel?

The Creative Bond (3/11)

Last fall my husband started building his seventh trike, just as I started writing the fifth book in the Detective Jackson series (my tenth novel altogether). *Dying for Justice* was released last week, and yesterday Steve took his first ride on the new trike.

Always having a creative project in the works is one of the bonding elements of our 23-year relationship. He listens while I talk about plots, publishing, and promotion, and I listen while he yaks about Type 1 Volkswagen engines, fiberglass bodies, and adjustable foot pegs. He reads my novels, and I take trike rides with him. I believe he gets the better deal, but I'm biased. Still, I think the three-wheeled motorcycles are so cool, I've given my main character, Detective Jackson, a trike-building hobby.

You wouldn't think a three-wheeled motorcycle and a crime fiction novel have much in common, but the creative process is surprisingly similar. Both start with a concept, a simple idea that each of us has been thinking about and can't wait to develop. For me, it could be a vivid opening scene or a character that sparks the whole novel. For him, it's often a type of engine or a new way to connect the two halves of his vehicle.

Next is the planning/designing phase. The first part of this process is all mental. We both spend a couple of weeks thinking about our projects, turning them over in our minds until they began to take shape. I can look at the expression on his face and know he's thinking about his next trike. *Honey, you're focused on your trike and haven't heard a word I've said, have you?* On the other hand, I do a lot of my brainstorming while I'm exercising. Those endorphins help produce some great plot twists!

Then the tangible planning takes place. For me, it means outlining. Determining and plotting, day-by-day, what happens in the story and in the investigation, then mapping it out in a Word document. For Steve, my trike builder, planning means drawings. He starts with a pencil drawing of the whole trike, then progresses to CAD versions of all the individual components, including dozens of parts for the frame alone. We each modify our plans as we go along, seeing what works and what doesn't.

Then he starts building and I start writing. For both of us, this is the hands-on work, the joy, and how we spend the bulk of our time. We're both happiest in the crafting phase. Of course, we have occasions when we get stuck. I'll realize a plot element doesn't work because of wrong timing and have to back up and revise. He'll recognize that two components don't fit together the way he envisioned, so he'll stop and redesign.

But it's just part of the process. We know from experience that we'll work through whatever glitches we encounter. In all our years, he's only abandoned one trike project, and I've only abandoned one novel. But my agent at the time discouraged me from it, and I may finish the thing yet.

I don't mean to imply we've always worked in tandem—in fact, we're often in different phases—but we do have a similar process and timetable. And eventually, we both end up with a finished product that we're proud of. Some people insist that what we both do is art, but we think of our projects as crafts...and now, small businesses.

Here's where the difference comes in. Steve sells each trike (or motorcycle) to a single individual to enjoy, and I sell my novels to thousands. But we both love what we do and can't imagine our lives without a project in the works. Sharing a creative compulsion is a big part of what keeps our relationship healthy.

How I Took Charge of My Life and Career (7/11)

In February 2010, I was laid off from our local newspaper, my second layoff in two years. I decided it was time to take charge of my life and career and to stop being someone else's employee, writing and publishing other people's stories, and getting let go when the work ran out. In my heart, I was a novelist, and it was time to make a living from my fiction. To get from point A to point B, I made some radical decisions.

I decided I had to stop wasting time and money on things that weren't working and focus on things that were. What wasn't working for me was my small publisher, which couldn't get my novels into bookstores. What was working for a lot of people was the growth of e-book sales.

I set aside the novel I was writing and got busy saving my career. The first step was to rewrite and self-publish on Kindle a standalone thriller I had completed but never sold. I'd once had a big-name agent for it, so I knew it was solid. I also had a second standalone thriller that my publisher had offered a contract for, but I hadn't signed it yet—because the book wasn't scheduled to be released until late 2012. That seemed like an eternal and foolish wait. I had a mortgage to pay immediately. What made sense was to get the two thrillers into the digital world where readers were buying. I took the second major step and let my publisher know I was withdrawing my standalone.

I spent a couple of months rewriting and updating the stories, then I paid for editing and cover design. I withdrew the money from my miniscule retirement account and considered it an investment in my future. That summer, I published the two thrillers (*The Baby*

Thief and *The Suicide Effect*) on Amazon's Kindle Direct Publishing. At that point, I had one foot in each world. I was self-published, but I still had a traditional press for my series.

Next, I rerouted my promotional efforts toward e-book readers. I quit sending marketing material to bookstores and instead joined several Kindle forums, where I participated in discussions. I got more active on Goodreads and did five back-to-back book giveaways just for the exposure. I wrote a dozen guest blogs and sent them all over the internet.

My sales jumped significantly. By then my publisher had uploaded the second Detective Jackson story (*Secrets to Die For*) to Kindle, and I started thinking about how much money I could make if my publisher wasn't keeping most of my digital profits.

After the third Jackson book (*Thrilled to Death*) faced the same difficulty getting into bookstores, I decided to withdraw from my press. It took a few weeks to finally make the call. Who willingly gives up a second publishing contract? Taking back my series meant foregoing the industry's stamp of approval. I hated to let it go, but I felt I had no choice if I wanted to make a living.

So I called my publisher and asked for my e-book rights back. I also asked to be released from the contract for the fourth Jackson story (*Passions of the Dead*). I knew the manuscript had not been edited, so no time or money had been invested. My publisher was not happy, but graciously granted my requests.

Letting go of that contract was one of the hardest things I've ever done. Not only did it mean taking on the *self-published* stigma, it also meant giving up book signings, which I love. But I had looked into the future and determined that bookstores were not where most people would buy their novels in 2012. For once, I wanted to be ahead of the curve.

I sent my Jackson files to be converted to e-books, then uploaded my versions to Amazon as my publisher took hers down. At that point, I had five books selling on Kindle, and my numbers were getting better every month. While the last manuscript was out for editing and cover design, I bought an inexpensive ad on the Kindle Nation newsletter and increased my online promotional efforts. Sales took another huge leap.

When I released the fourth Jackson story on Kindle, I dropped the price of the first book in the series (*The Sex Club*), to $.99. Sales for the first book skyrocketed, and a week later, sales for the follow-up stories nearly doubled.

Mystery Scene and *Crimespree* magazines gave me great reviews, lending credibility to my work, and devoted readers spread the word. By the end of the year, my series was a bestseller on Kindle, and I was making a living from my novels. I now have seven books on the market, an eighth coming out in September, and no worries about being laid off. Taking charge of my writing career and investing in myself was the best thing I've ever done.

Chapter 2: The Writing Life

Taking the Plunge (4/08)

At the end of last year, I decided that 2008 would be different. I had several goals:

1) Start a new novel.

2) Work on my novel first thing every day, even if I had to get up an hour earlier.

3) Find or create paying work that I enjoyed more than what I was currently doing to earn a living.

4) Sell my detective series to another publisher.

By March first, I had accomplished the three things I had control over—although not the way I expected to. January first, I began to outline my new Detective Jackson novel with the working title, *Secrets to Die For*. I began getting up at five o'clock to write for an hour before I went to work. At the time, I worked as an editor for an educational publisher, a demanding job that left me too mentally exhausted at the end of the day to feel creative enough to fill blank page after blank page.

Next, I started sending out letters to agents, publishers, and writers, announcing my services as a fiction editor. And I contacted some corporate clients and magazines about nonfiction editing as well. Then I took the biggest step: I asked my employer to let me cut back on my hours at work, thinking it would be a long slow transition to self-employment. They promptly laid me off.

Terrified, but joyously liberated, I plunged into a new routine: Write for three or four hours exclusively on my novel first thing every morning, break for an hour of exercise, then freelance edit for others. And the work poured in—enough to pay the bills. Now in the evenings, instead of trying to squeeze in a little bit of uninspired writing, I have time to network and market my novel that's currently in print. Most days I'm at my desk from six in the morning until ten at night, but very little of it feels like work.

I love my new life! My bathroom is perpetually untidy, dinner is often an unimaginative freezer-to-oven meal, and there's laundry backed up everywhere. But yesterday, I passed page 150 on my novel, so who cares? My husband says he's never seen me so happy. It's the first time in my life that I've put my personal writing first. Making a living, raising kids, taking care of extended family, and keeping the house together were always the priorities. These things are still important, but they are no longer most important. (Don't call child services; my kids are adults now.)

My goal is to keep it going for as long as possible—because I finally feel like my real self. I know that not every writer is in a position to make this kind of change, but I heartily recommend it if you can.

A Day in the Life of an Aspiring Novelist (12/08)

9:42 am: As I write page 162, I realize that an entire investigative thread in my new novel is not quite logical. And there's no way to massage it or spin it. So I go back to the beginning and try to pick out and rewrite every reference to this plot line. Did I get them all? Or did I leave a little sliver of foreign material that will pop up and irritate readers? Now I have doubts about other plot threads. So I decide to print out all 162 pages and read through them before continuing to write the story. How many trees have I killed in my career as a writer and editor?

12:29 am: Another writer posts on my Facebook page, *Congrats on the review in Mystery Scene. "A thrilling, eye-opening read."* I am excited. I haven't seen this review, and it will make a great blurb. I search *Mystery Scene's* webpage, but I can't find the review and I don't have a copy of the magazine. So everyone in the mystery community knows what this review says, except me. And, of course, I worry that the one line I know about may be the only positive thing the reviewer said.

3:10 pm: After months of waiting, my beta reader sends an email with her feedback on the first 50 pages of my new story, *Secrets to Die For*. After commenting, "This is a very worthy story, a page-turner with great potential," she says, "Try to SHOW rather than TELL." Aaaghhhhh! I like to think I live by this ubiquitous writing rule. But now I wonder: Do I even know what I'm doing?

6:17 pm: After months of waiting, the book trailer for my recently published novel, *The Sex Club*, arrives via email. I excitedly click open the file, ready to be thrilled and amazed. But no, the trailer is weird and confusing. The girl in the last scene is at least 20, dark-haired, and kind of heavy. She doesn't even look dead. The victim in my novel is 14, blond and thin, and very dead. I show the trailer to my husband. He hates almost everything about it and cannot stop talking about how much he dislikes it. I am crushed. I spent the last of my promotional money on the trailer, and I counted on it selling a few books. Now I have to compose an email that diplomatically says, "Start over." It takes an hour that I don't have.

9:05 pm: I receive an email from a mystery book club leader named Ruth Greiner, who apparently does have a copy of the *Mystery Scene* review and says she'll never read *The Sex Club* no matter how great all the reviews are. She does not say why, and she does not have to. Just seeing her name horrified me. The antagonist in *The Sex Club* is a very nasty woman and her name is Ruth Greiner. How was I to know? Now I have to write an email that explains how I chose the name—Ruth Biblical and strong, Greiner is the name of a street in my old neighborhood. I also try to carefully express my concern for her feelings, but without admitting any liability. I offer to send her a free copy of my next novel, then feel lame about it.

10:16 pm: Yet another fun-filled email arrives. This one is from a local author whom I met at a book fair and exchanged novels with. He says he's quite sure he'll find a publisher for his new novel and wants to know if I'll read his book and write a blurb for the front cover. This is the first time anyone has asked me for a blurb, and I'd like to be excited. I'm flattered that he thinks I have any clout. But I didn't get past the first page of his first novel—which started with a rectal search by a large German woman—and this one, he says, is much more sexually explicit. How do I get so lucky? Oh yea, I wrote a novel called *The Sex Club*, so he must think I'm a sex fiend. (It's a mystery/thriller, really!) So far, his email is just sitting there, unanswered. But tomorrow is another day, and I'm a creative person. I'll think of something.

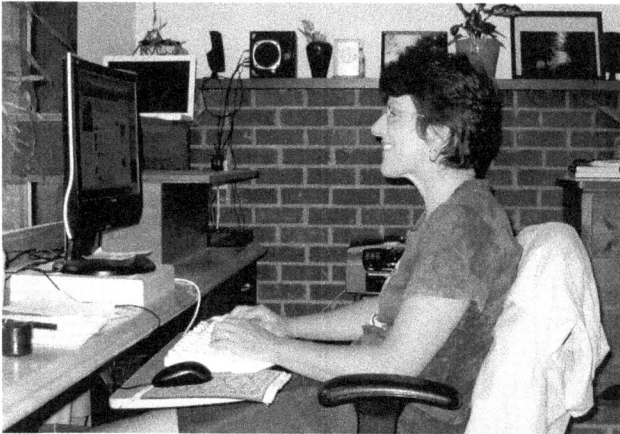

My First Book Club Discussion (7/08)

This morning I participated in my first discussion with a mystery book club, the Rocky Mountain Readers of Colorado Springs. It was great fun, and would only have been better if I could have met these delightful women in person. I'll recap our discussion of *The Sex Club* here:

How did you come to write this story? My stories always reflect issues, events, or cultural changes that are currently on my mind. In this case, there were several. Years ago, there was news of a large group of middle school students spreading syphilis among themselves and engaging in orgies. This rather shocked me, and I'm not easily shocked. Then our own government starting spending taxpayers' money to teach abstinence-only sex education, which seemed like such a bad idea. Then there's my own personal belief that trying to suppress sex among teenagers (or any group) will almost always backfire. And, in general, I had noticed a rise in violence among teenage girls. I kept thinking about these events/issues and wondering if they were connected or how I could connect them to create a compelling story.

Why did you pick *The Sex Club* as a title? This subject has generated more discussion than anything else about the book. As I was writing the story, which I had yet to name, Kera at one point referred to the group of sexually active girls as "the sex club." And I had one of those moments and thought: *That's it. That the right name.* My husband had doubts, but I didn't listen to him. (Rarely do.) I admit, the marketer in me thought the name would grab readers' attention. But as it turns out, some mystery readers are not crazy about the name, and the women in this group said they were embarrassed about asking for the book in the library and bookstore. But they all loved it, anyway.

Who did the orange panties belong to? I love it when readers pay attention to all the little details and want to know how every piece of the evidence plays into the story. So I'm careful not to leave loose ends. But in reality, that sometimes happens in police work, and some questions are never answered. But I won't provide an explanation here, because some of you (actually, millions of you) haven't read the book yet.

Was the mayor telling the truth? This would be a major spoiler for the uninitiated, and I purposely left this ambiguous in the story so readers could decide for themselves. Clearly, it made no difference in terms of his punitive consequences, and this is often how our judicial system works.

In the next story, do Kera and Jackson get to have sex? You will simply have to read the next Detective Jackson story, *Secrets to Die For*, to find out. (But keep in mind the name of my first novel.)

The Worst Thing About Being a Novelist (8/08)

As I opened my email this morning and read through the new mystery listserv postings, the theme was *July Reads*. At first I thought, I could post about this. Then I realized it wouldn't be much of an offering. I didn't actually finish a single book last month. I started several but lost interest and put them down. (More about that phenomenon tomorrow.) But I don't lack for novels to read. I have a huge TBR (to be read) pile.

For me, the worst thing about being a novelist is the lack of time to read novels! Before I started writing stories, I read at least one or two books a week. Now I feel lucky if I can read 10 novels a year. And it kills me. Especially when I meet other mystery/crime authors. I'd love to be able to say, "I read your new novel and I loved it." But most of the time, I haven't read any of their work.

I don't know how to get around this. I've given up what little TV I used to watch and that has helped some. But still, working as an editor, writing new novels, promoting my published novel, online networking, and spending time with family uses up almost every minute of every day. And the only one of those activities that I'd give up voluntarily is my editing job. But then I'd end up homeless. So not having enough fiction-reading time is a painful sacrifice I have to make, and I don't see that changing any time soon.

As a novelist, I read fiction differently now too. The author's choices—POV, pacing, foreshadowing, syntax—are always present. It's much harder to simply be absorbed into a story and transported away for hours the way I used to. Sometimes I think that being an avid reader (back in the day) was more fun than being a novelist. But there's no going back. I am a storyteller now; it defines me.

The 2nd Worst Thing About Being a Novelist (8/08)

I mentioned yesterday that now as a novelist I read differently than I did before I starting writing fiction. I am aware of POV changes (subtle and not), plot devices, foreshadowing, pacing, and more. Noticing these things often makes me stop and think, *Why did the author do that?* I am also extremely busy and have to make time to read, so if a book doesn't grab me—or makes me stop too often to think about the author—I put it in the giveaway pile and move on. Consequently, I only finish one out of every three or four novels I start. (Which is why I almost never buy hardback books, but that's another subject.) I don't mean to imply that all these books are bad or unreadable, they just weren't right for me.

Also as a novelist, I'm trying to get to know and network with other writers. I've made many friends online, and I look forward to meeting all these nice-funny-interesting people in person at conferences. But here's the sticky part: What do I say if they ask me if I liked their novel and it was one of those I put down? Social training tells me to tell a little white lie and quickly change the subject: "Great writing. What are you working on now?" (I have also taken a vow to never ask anyone that question about my own work.)

Here's the trickier part. I'm a member of several mystery discussion groups, the point of which is to discuss books we've read. Other novelists are also members of these groups. How do I discuss a novel I didn't really care for without offending or alienating the author who may be reading my posts? And what if I signed up to be the moderator for the discussion— before I read the book? Which means I can't just sit back and be quiet. I face this dilemma today. I'm supposed to discuss a book I haven't finished. Technically, there's nothing wrong with it. The writing is good and many people would find the character compelling. I just don't care for gun-toting, hard-drinking, wise-ass men. Or stories about the mob. Being the kind of person who can be counted on to do what I say, I'll finish the book, post intelligent questions, and try to be as diplomatic as possible with my own opinions.

But I won't volunteer to moderate any more discussions unless I've already read the book and loved it. Or the author is no longer living.

Outrageous Agent Contest (8/08)

In honor of all the hardworking agents in this business, I'm holding a contest today for the most outrageous story about a writer's experience with an agent. The winner gets a copy of my novel, or if you already have my novel, I'll host you on my blog—whoopee! Being a good host, I'll go first.

In August 2003, I attended a writers' conference and pitched two novels to an agent I'll call *Susie Strange*. You can name your agent, if you'd like. I have good reason not to. She loved both pitches and asked to see full manuscripts for both novels, which I happened to have with me. So off she went to NY with 170,000 words of mine. I waited the customary two months, then sent an email. No response. I eventually sent another email and made a phone call with absolutely no acknowledgment that I even existed. But this is not the bizarre part.

I went on with my life and wrote yet another novel called *The Sex Club*. As I neared the end of process, I started sending out agent query letters, with three chapters included—knowing how long it takes them to respond. I sent one (on a whim) to Susie Strange. You know the opening: *We met once at a conference …* The date on that Word document is October 21, 2004.

A year later, I signed with a different agent, spent another year working with her on the story, then she failed to sell it. Then I spent another year or so bringing it to print through a niche publisher, followed by months of promoting it.

Then on February 7, 2008, I received a call from someone in Susy Strange's agency. I didn't recognize the caller's name, but I knew the agency. She said she had read the first three chapters of *The Sex Club* and wanted to see the entire manuscript. I was confused at first. "What do you mean you want to see the manuscript? It's a published book." Then it hit me. She was responding to the query I had sent THREE YEARS AND THREE MONTHS before!

The poor woman was new to the agency and had inherited an old slush pile, but she handled the situation gracefully. She asked if I was working on anything else and agreed to read the first 50 pages of *Secrets to Die For*. She got back to me within three weeks and said she loved it. Now she's waiting for me to send the entire manuscript. As much as I want to be represented, the idea of working with her makes me a little nervous. After all, she is a protégée of Susy Strange.

First, the poll: Should I send it to her? Should I send it to other agents as well?

Second, the contest: Can you top that outrageous agent story?

Staying Sane While Working at Home (6/09)

My commute was up the stairs. My workday was self-directed, flexible, and light on responsibility. Most people would call it the ideal job. For me, working at home for a magazine was a long slow descent into depression, anxiety, and claustrophobia. The rest of the magazine staff was in New York, and a week at a time would pass without a call from my co-workers. Emails simply served to exchange files. I was alone for eight or nine hours a day for more than a year and it drove me insane. I am a social creature. I generate energy from being around people. But that period in my life was years ago, before Facebook, Twitter, and listservs.

Now I'm working at home again as a novelist and freelance editor. So far, I'm loving it. But it's different this time. I'm connected to people through the internet, and I'm able to set my own hours and take breaks when I want. But I worry about what it will be like for me six months or a year from now. I want this career phase to work out long term. So here's my strategy for staying sane while working at home:

1. Make time to reach out to people on the internet, periodically throughout the day.

2. Have lunch with a real-live person once a week.

3. Conduct interviews in person even if they can be done by phone.

4. Schedule regular social activities (such as weekly bowling with my brothers).

5. Join a writers group and meet periodically (I haven't done this yet, but it's on my list).

6. Open Pandora, click my funk station, and dance for five minutes at least twice a day. Dancing is so joyful, it wards off depression.

A Life of Uncertainty (10/08)

If I were a widget maker who went to work in a factory at the same time every day, I would leave work at the same time and the collect the same paycheck. There would be no uncertainty.

Instead, I'm a novelist and freelance editor. No two days are alike, and uncertainty is a way of life. Will this novel I'm writing sell to a publisher? After spending 25 hours on this manuscript, will the writer actually send me a check? Will I have enough freelance work this month to pay my mortgage?

A little background: I'm a Type A personality and a bit of a control freak. I never leave on a road trip without a map and a reservation. I am not made for uncertainty.

And yet, the life of a widget maker would drive me insane. Conversely, I love this life as a novelist and freelancer. So I must learn to live with uncertainty. Some days are easier than others. Yesterday got the best of me. Financially, this is the worst year my husband and I have ever had, and things will get worse before they get better. But in some ways, we are happier than ever.

Financial insecurity is not the worst of it though. The question of whether my completed novel will sell sometimes hinders my ability to move forward. I have a new novel outlined and two chapters written, yet a little part of my brain says, *Why bother?*

I have always managed to push past this point, although it once took a few years And I will again. I write because I am a storyteller. And the life of a storyteller is always filled with uncertainty.

A Limited Number of Words (9/09)

Is there a finite number of words that each writer can produce—within each week or month or lifetime? Some writers seem prolific no matter what, but for myself, I think I have periodic limits. Last year, I worked about the same number of non-novel (meaning, paid) hours as I have this year and yet I still managed to write a novel and a half. This year, my novel writing word count has tapered off drastically, and I'm even blogging a lot less too.

Why? Last year I was doing mostly editing for a living. This year I'm mostly writing for the newspaper. Conclusion: The paper is getting my writing juice, the bulk of my words. And apparently, the supply is limited. My husband would argue that only applies to written, not spoken, volume.

This is an odd predicament to be in. In many ways, the newspaper position is the perfect part-time job. All I have to do is write feature stories, which I enjoy. No other responsibilities, and a dependable pay check. It's an easy, fun job. How can I complain?

But I want to write novels. Excuse me, I should have said, I **need** to write novels. It's not about what I should be doing. It's what I must do, if I want to be truly happy.

Meanwhile, I'm putting in more hours than usual at the paper and struggling to work on my novel every morning before work and on weekends. The blogging will continue to get the short end, and I have to make peace with that. I only have so many words.

Is working in non-writing fields actually better for your novels?

The Writer's Dilemma (9/09)

About ten years into my fiction writing adventure, I read an interview that changed my life. The featured scriptwriter had recently sold his first screenplay, which was made into a blockbuster movie. When the interviewer asked him if he would do anything differently, given the chance, he said, "If I had known it would take ten years to sell a script, I would have found a better day job."

That hit home with me, and I knew I had to make a change. At the time, I had been waiting tables for years while my kids were young (for the flexibility), and I was starting to really hate it...and myself. Novel writing in my spare time was all that kept me sane. I had also recently failed to sell a novel even though my agent told me we had an offer. In that somewhat despondent frame of mind, I decided I needed a better day job. One that would put my journalism degree and inquisitive mind to work—for pay. I realized that the time I spent at work also counted on the happiness meter and that working a job I hated and that made me feel bad about myself was not in my best interest in the long term.

So I stopped living for the future—that day when a novel would sell and my life would change. I found a job on a magazine, and I accepted, on some level, that magazine writing and editing would be my career and that it would be enough if that's how it all worked out. It was a great job with eventually great pay, and it led to even better jobs with better pay. It was the best move I ever made.

Or maybe it was the worst.

Of course I kept writing novels. For many of us, it's like a drug. Once you're hooked, there's no stopping, no true happiness without that fix. But over the years of working for various nonfiction publishers, I wrote less and less in my free time. It took longer and longer to finish a novel. I wrote screenplays for a while because they were easier and needed fewer words. So it took another ten years to finally get a contract and get the first two novels in a mystery/suspense series published. And I had to lose my job first.

Looking back, I see that the only prolific novel-writing periods I've had were during layoffs. I wrote *The Sex Club* after the magazine moved to NY, and I wrote *Secrets to Die For* and most of the third novel, *Thrilled to Death*, after my lay off last year when the recession hit.

I've come to conclude that I have a limited number of words I can produce each week or month, a finite capacity for intellectual creativity.

Now I've come full circle. I'm writing for a newspaper and working more hours than originally expected. (Unemployment doesn't last forever, and it's tough to make real money as a new novelist.) The newspaper job is ideal. All I do is write feature stories; I have no other responsibilities. I don't even have to attend meetings, and my boss thinks I'm terrific.

Guess what? My novel word count has slowly plummeted, and I'm feeling a little cranky about it. (I started the fourth story in the Detective Jackson series in June, and I'm only at 15,000 words!) I think sometimes that my novel-writing career would be better served if I worked a job that didn't require me to write. But I'm afraid that any other kind of job would make me feel like I wasn't living up to my potential, that I was wasting my education and skills.

What will I do? Beats me. I know I'm not going back to waiting tables! If I stall long enough on making a decision, the paper will make it for me and lay me off. We're down 150 staff members, with only 250 to go. I'm almost hoping it will happen sooner rather than later.

Many other novelists are also journalists or technical writers or they work in communications of some kind. I suspect they also face this word-count conundrum, and I sympathize.

Loving the Moment (1/10)

If you're wondering what I've been up to lately, in four short words: I'm having a blast. Much of it has to do with my newspaper job. In the last few months, I've interviewed cartoonist Jan Eliot, a professor of film studies who discussed great women movie characters, a 77-year-old woman doing standup with a very naughty routine, and a female weightlifting champion, to name a few. As a novelist, I've been privileged to interview a crime lab supervisor, a SWAT sergeant, a homicide detective, an internal investigations detective, and another novelist. I've also been interviewed by several other novelists.

I feel so fortunate to make all these connections and have so many terrific people share what they know with me. Jan Eliot is bright and engaging and generously shared her travel experiences with me for a newspaper story. Local readers contacted me to say how much they loved the story. Jan also read my first book, *The Sex Club,* and loved it. Patrice, the standup comic, is now hanging out with my mother, and hopefully wearing off on her a little. And I'm pleased to have another contact at the university, where I hope to work someday.

All the law enforcement people I've met are great resources who will gladly answer questions for me as I write. In addition, one of the detectives I interviewed wrote a script based on a very prominent case here in Eugene involving dirty cops who raped vulnerable women. He asked me to read his script and give him feedback. Not only is the script well done, it's filled with inside details that the public never knew at the time. I feel so honored that he trusted me with his work...and his secrets.

I'm also writing author profiles now for *The Big Thrill,* so I get to interview and write about other novelists. Love it! My first interview was with Julie Compton, author of *Tell No Lies* and *Rescuing Olivia.*

Left Coast Crime is coming up soon too, and it will be another opportunity to meet writers and readers and reconnect with people I've met at previous conferences. For me, the notion of a writer, alone at her desk in a life of solitude, couldn't be farther from the truth. Meeting people is the best part of my writing life!

New Day, New Direction (2/10)

I'm a free agent again. In other words, I've been laid off my part-time newspaper job. The weirdest part? I received an unemployment debit card from the state last week. I laughed and twittered: *Do they know something I don't?* I guess they did.

The hardest part? Walking away from a terrific group of people I've come to really enjoy and count on for emotional and intellectual interaction. The good news is the paper will give me freelance work, and I'll meet with my writer/editor friends every once in while.

This is my third layoff in publishing in the last five years, so I'm not devastated. The layoffs were all economic decisions, and I have glowing letters of recommendation from everyone. I know I'll come out okay. In the mean time, I'll get caught up on my promotional list and finish the edits on three novels. Yes, I have three books being released in the next 18 months. So there should be royalty checks coming too. Not to mention the overwhelming excitement of having so much of my work out there!

Life is good. I knew the job was temporary when I started, and it was great for me in many ways. I'm better known now in my community as a person, a journalist, and a novelist. I've met a lot of terrific people and worked on some fun stories.

I plan to do more fiction editing and blogging— offering writing, promoting, and organizational advice, so stop back in regularly. I love to hear from everyone, and if you've had a similar experience, feel free to share it here.

Writing the Right Thing at the Right Time (7/10)

I've changed my mind again. The futuristic thriller is on hold and I just wrote the opening lines for the fifth book in my Detective Jackson series. My fans (all 13 of them) will be happy, and I'm feeling quite relieved myself. I still plan to write *The Arranger* (set in 2023) but I'm not in the right space to do it now.

It's hard for me to admit something is too challenging, but that's the truth of this situation. Because I'm still a full-time freelance editor, as well as a novelist and book marketer, I have a lot going on. I feel overwhelmed most days and my writing time is limited to mornings only. Being creative moments after waking up is challenging enough without trying to write a novel that is outside my comfort zone. That's part of the reason I wanted to do it, but I'm making such slow progress that it feels like not writing at all.

So I'm setting the futuristic thriller aside for next year when I hope to have more time and focus to write. My priority right now is to get to a point where I'm actually making money from my novels and can give up some of the freelance work.

Which is why I've been in revision/edit mode all year, another reason the novel wasn't moving forward. First I had to write and submit the second draft of *Passions of the Dead* (Jackson #4). Then I worked through line edits from my publisher for *Thrilled to Death* (Jackson #3), which launches in print soon. I also worked through line edits of *The Baby Thief*, a standalone thriller that will publish next year and possibly sooner as an e-book.

If that weren't enough, I decided to dig out a thriller I wrote years ago and revise it. That took time and focus. The plan is to publish *The Suicide Effect* on Kindle as early as next week. Now that Amazon is paying a 70% royalty, the income from this book will take me a step closer to my goal of making a living as a novelist.

It's possible my publisher will release it as a print book someday. It's also quite likely that print books will become less and less of a consideration when I think about my future as a novelist.

Readers: When series authors take time off to write standalones, do you get frustrated waiting for the next series book? Do you try their standalones?

The Fear Factor (5/11)

In my personal life I try to be optimistic, but in my fiction I write about my fears. It's been true since I sat down to write my first novel. At the time, Jeffrey Dahmer was in the news and my greatest fear was that a sexual predator would kidnap and kill one of my three young boys. So I wrote a story about a woman who tracks down her son's killer. The experience was cathartic, and I continued the practice in future novels, because as it turns out, many readers share the same fears.

Being kidnapped and held against my will is another dominant fear for me and millions of other women as well—because it happens!—so the theme occurs often in crime fiction novels, including two of mine (*The Baby Thief, Secrets to Die For*). Most of my stories though have elements of fears that are very personal to me. For example, when I wrote *The Sex Club*, the first book in the Detective Jackson series, my son was in Iraq and I worried constantly that he would die. My sister had just succumbed to cancer and I grieved for her and worried for other members of my family. So Kera, my main female protagonist, was dealing with those elements. Right or wrong, I couldn't separate those emotions from my writing and they ended up on the page.

Soon after that, my husband was diagnosed with retroperitoneal fibrosis, which triggered all kinds of fears for me. He faced a life of pain, multiple surgeries, and likely an early death. Without being consciously aware that I was doing it at first, my Jackson character started having pain and health issues. Eventually, he was diagnosed with RF, and in *Thrilled to Death,* he underwent a surgery, very similar to the one my husband experienced. Readers tell me they enjoy characters who are realistic, yet unique, so incorporating true-to-life, frightening details adds richness to my stories while helping me work through emotional challenges.

In late 2009 when I was writing *Passions of the Dead*, I was dealing with unemployment: mine, my husband's, my brother's, and dozens of other people I knew. I witnessed the devastating effect it can have on families. That theme became dominant when I outlined the story. My Jackson novels are always about crime, murder in particular, and my main goal is tell a great story. But every fictitious crime needs a unique, complex, and compelling motive, and I look for those motives in the fear I'm experiencing.

Some of my fears are more social and universal. I fear that as a society we have wrongfully imprisoned hundreds, if not thousands, of innocent people. Dozens of news stories about the release of prisoners wrongfully convicted continue to feed this fear, so the issue is part of the plot in *Dying for Justice*, the fifth Detective Jackson novel.

Right now I fear for the future of our country if the economy doesn't improve. I also fear for our comfort and safety if the extreme weather patterns continue and grow worse. So I'm writing a futuristic thriller in which those fears come into play. Guilt and redemption are also prominent themes in *The Arranger*, which will release in early September.

Soon I'll start work on the next Jackson book. I have a list of ideas, many culled from true crime cases found in the news. Regardless of what I decide in the beginning though, you can bet that as the plot develops, whatever fear is most prevalent on my mind will surface in the story.

What are your greatest fears? What fears do you like to read about?

Chapter 3: The Jackson Series

The Hobgoblin of Little Minds (9/10)

Ralph Waldo Emerson reportedly said, "A foolish consistency is the hobgoblin of little minds." He clearly wasn't writing a mystery series.

Kindle readers have suddenly discovered my Detective Jackson series, and many are reading my stories back to back. This can be a dangerous thing. When the details of previous stories are fresh in their minds, readers are so much more likely to catch inconsistencies. So far, none have contacted me to complain about anything serious, but other authors haven't faired as well. For example, this forum post by a ticked off reader caught my attention.

She doesn't bother to keep the non-main characters' backstories straight. The mayor of the small town is a female obstetrician in book one, and by book three or four has become a male car salesman. The ex-girlfriend originally has a mother with whom the protagonist has had dinner, but in a later book she is an orphan who recently lost her only sister. Oops!

This complaint is about a mega-bestselling author, and these inconsistencies obviously haven't cost her much. But as an upcoming writer, I believe I can't afford to make these kind of mistakes.

During the writing of Jackson book two, *Secrets to Die For*, I kept searching the manuscript of the first Jackson story looking for specific detail, and I realized I needed to start a file to track these things. So I created an Excel document and started copying/pasting details into character columns right after I typed them. Parents' names, make of car, cell phone ring tone—anything attached to a character I added to my character database. At least that's how it works in theory.

I didn't know I was writing a series when I penned the first Jackson story, so I didn't start this file from the beginning. I wish I had. A secondary character who appeared in book one came back in book three with a different hair color. I keep expecting more of these little quirks to surface, but I'm doing everything I can now to avoid it.

Readers also follow character development more closely than I realized. Several people have contacted me to ask: *What happened to Kera's ex-husband? He disappeared in book three.* As the author, I let go of that particular conflict because I'd given the main characters a new family member to struggle with. But readers hadn't forgotten and wanted to see a more thorough wrap-up.

That complaint pales in comparison to what readers have posted about lack of character development from other authors. Here's a sample.

You would think, for example, that by book four the chief of police might pay a little more attention to a guy who has sussed out no less than three murders originally thought to be accidents/suicides (in a small town, in a less-than-six-month timeframe) but no, he continues to dismiss all opinions as fantasy. The protagonist has some kind of interest in three different women over the course of the series, but the relationships don't really develop either sexually or as friendships.

It's not that readers want characters to be static. They want protagonists to grow and change, but in a natural and logical way that comes from the story. If the protagonist is exactly the same from book to book, no matter what happens to her, readers get bored and give up the series. So writers must achieve a fine balance and create subtle, organic changes.

It's good to know readers take our work seriously enough to care and comment. If our characters didn't seem believable, these issues wouldn't matter. As a writer, I want my characters to come across so realistic that everything about them makes sense to the reader. Even the little details I didn't think would count. It's challenging but worth it.

The Fourth Jackson Story Is Released (10/10)

To celebrate the launch of my fourth Jackson story, *Passions of the Dead*, the first book in the series, *The Sex*

Club is now only $.99 as an e-book. For those who have never tried the series, here's the short blurb for the first book:

The Sex Club: A dead girl, a ticking bomb, a Bible study that is not what it appears to be, and a detective who won't give up.

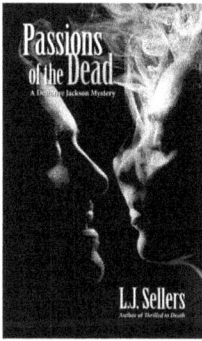

For those who are keeping up with the series, here's the back cover copy for **Passions of the Dead**: A working-class family is brutally attacked in their home and only one survives. Detective Jackson is assigned to investigate and soon uncovers a blackmail scheme. But the forensic evidence is confusing, and the girl who survives has no memory of the horrific event. When another home invasion occurs, Jackson is confident they've nailed the perpetrators. Yet the case grows even more entangled. When the survivor disappears, Jackson fears for her life—but can he find her in time to save her?

It's available as an e-book in all formats for $2.99 and in print from Amazon.

I'm deeply grateful for the opportunity to do what I love—write this series—and I'm grateful for the enthusiastic support from my readers!

Detective Jackson's Detour

The fifth book in the Detective Jackson series, *Dying for Justice*, is a little different from the others, and I wanted to share the background for how this story developed. I outlined the plot in February of last year. At that time, I planned to give up the series because the second book had a failed launch and I worried that I was facing yet another failure with the same publisher. I had two more Jackson books written, with one under contract. I thought if I could launch a different series with a new character and a new publisher, I might be able to save my career. So I mapped out a plot in which Detective Evans, one of Jackson's sidekicks, was the lead character with Jackson as a strong secondary character—hoping my old readers would come along with the new series.

Then everything changed. My husband and I were laid off our jobs, e-books started to take off, and I re-envisioned my novelist career. I set the new police procedural aside to rewrite two standalone thrillers and put them up on Kindle. Next I regained the rights to my series and self-published the first four Jackson books. That took most of the year.

In October, my series became a bestseller on Kindle and readers were asking for more Jackson novels. At that point, I was finally ready to start writing again. After reading through my outline for the Evans-based story, I decided I really liked the plot and would go ahead and write it, giving the two detectives equal POV roles.

So my latest Jackson story also features Detective Evans as a major POV character. She and Jackson each work their own homicide cases and tell their own stories...which of course come to overlap in a stunning twist.

Every story I write is based, at least partially, on a social issue I'm feeling strongly about at the time. When I conceptualized this plot, I couldn't stop thinking about prisoners who had been released after their convictions were overturned. In several cases, the suspect had been coerced into a false confession. I felt compelled to highlight the issue, and in book four, *Passions of the Dead*, I'd mentioned that Jackson's parents had been murdered and the killer had gone to jail. It was the perfect opening for a novel involving a false confession. I worried that having Jackson reopen and solve his parents' case would seem cliché, but it's only one element of the story. Detective Evans also works a case from the past and her main suspect is a police sergeant. The overlapping stories are powerful, and readers have responded incredibly well to the novel.

The other theme in *Dying for Justice* is the issue of family estrangement. I'm very close to my own siblings who all live here in Eugene. But my husband went for years without talking to his brothers, and I've discovered that the phenomenon is fairly common. I wrote about this issue to help me understand how it can happen to families.

Using two protagonists and cases made the story challenging at times, but I had a blast writing from

Evans' POV. She's very different from Jackson—more physical, more impatient, more impulsive—and it was liberating to let her out in full action. In fact, once I developed Evans' character more fully, I liked her enough to bring her forward into the futuristic thriller I'm writing now. My hope is that basing this standalone book on a familiar character will bring my Jackson readers along for the ride.

The Evolution of Lara Evans (7/11)

My protagonist, Lara Evans, came into existence in 2005 when I wrote *The Sex Club*, the first book in the Detective Jackson series. She was one of the investigators on Jackson's taskforce, but Lara didn't have a POV role and readers didn't learn much about her. Over the next few books, readers learned a little more—that she was smart, had once been a paramedic, and that her relationships were temporary and mostly physical.

But readers didn't get inside her head until book four, *Passions of the Dead*. I gave her a few short POV sections, and fans learned that Lara had a crush on Jackson. One of my early readers penned this note in the margin: *I knew it! This will be interesting.*

In the fifth book, *Dying for Justice,* Lara took a central role as one of the main POV characters who solves the crimes and makes a daring arrest. As I wrote from

Lara's POV for long sections, she became special to me. I had so much fun writing about this kick-ass woman I knew I had to feature her more in future books. Interestingly enough, I'd been thinking about writing a futuristic thriller, a genre I love to read, but had never experimented with as an author.

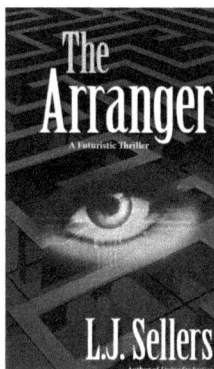

One day I was watching paramedics haul someone out of a house, and I envisioned a whole opening scene with paramedics witnessing a crime at one of their calls and becoming a target for killers. From that scene, *The Arranger* was born. Conveniently enough, my character Lara had once worked as a paramedic, and I was excited to bring her forward into the story. So my once-minor character became a driving force in my next plot.

The Arranger is set 13 years in the future, and Lara is no longer a detective because of a tragic mistake. She's working as a freelance paramedic in a bleak new world and training to compete in the Gauntlet. Developing the intense competition was a direct result of the kind of person Lara is. She's high energy and an adrenaline junkie. She runs, kickboxes, and climbs walls at the gym. She's obsessed with self-defense because of a series of assaults she's suffered, one as a college student and one as an officer in *Dying for Justice*. She's highly sexual, but needs more from a relationship, and she's often attracted to men in uniform.

Lara was the perfect character to bring into *The Arranger*, and the story developed partially because of who she is. Ideally, all novels should work that way, with plot and character developing concomitantly.

People ask me if there will be a sequel or series starring more of "future Lara." I honestly don't know yet. I love writing Lara's character, so I wouldn't be surprised to see her back for more adventures.

Chapter 4: Characters in Fiction

Sleazy Protagonists

Alcoholics, sex addicts, porn stars, thieves, and kidnappers. In today's crime fiction, these characters are often the protagonists, and as a reader, I'm expected to root for them. I rarely can. I've put down many well written and well plotted novels lately because the main character was not someone I could relate to.

For example, in one story, the protagonist—a reformed criminal, living a good life—participated in a kidnapping to keep himself from going to jail. If I had not been reading the book for discussion, I would have put it down immediately. I skimmed through the rest, uncaring. For me, there was little point in reading about a protagonist I wanted to see caught and punished. Especially since I predicted the book wouldn't turn out that way (and it didn't).

In another story, the character was well developed, resourceful, and good-hearted and I really wanted to like her. But the world she inhabited was sleazy, and everyone she encountered gave me the creeps. Despite the terrific writing, I finally gave up, because spending too much time in her world was a little revolting.

Don't get me wrong. I love crime fiction! And I'm certainly not a prude. I write a mystery/suspense series, and the first book is called *The Sex Club*. My main character is a homicide detective who's a hardworking family man. Not perfect, by any means, but he's also not a cynical, pill-popping alcoholic with dysfunctional relationships. I'm tired of that cop stereotype, and I want my character to be someone readers can relate to.

But it's not a clear-cut issue for me either. Two of my favorite books this year had protagonists who were criminals...or at least they had been. In *Beat the Reaper*, the main character is an ex-hit man who becomes a doctor. But he's trying to redeem himself, and it's a terrific and often funny story. *The Lock Artist*, another novel I loved, is about a psychologically mute safecracker. But the reader knows from the beginning that Michael goes to jail and hopes to change his life. So I rooted for both characters all the way.

For me, good characterization for a protagonist, especially a recurring character, means creating someone readers will care about, like, and/or respect in some way. I make an exception for Elmore Leonard's stories, in which everyone is shady, but often likeable, and I can always cheer for a charming thief, especially if he's played by George Clooney.

I realize I may be somewhat alone in this thinking (except for the George Clooney part). In my book discussion groups, many other readers say they don't have to like the protagonist to find the story compelling.

How do you feel about protagonists who are unlikable, deeply flawed, or simply not someone you'd ever spend time with? Can you name a novel you thoroughly enjoyed even though you didn't like the protagonist?

What Makes a Character Great?

I've been thinking about characters lately, mostly about how to make them more compelling. So I asked: Who are my favorite fictional police detectives? I came up with Lucas Davenport (John Sandford's Prey series) and April Woo (by Leslie Glass). I thought I might find commonalities that attract me as a reader. Instead, I discovered they are very different.

Davenport seems to have no family, no parents or siblings that he is connected to in any way. April Woo has parents who are very present in her life. Davenport has a lot of money and doesn't need to work. Woo has money problems, mostly because of her parents. Davenport knows how to play the political game to get what he wants out of the department. Woo is incapable of playing politics and lacks social skills in general.

So why do I like both these characters? Perhaps because they are both independent and unconcerned with what others think of them. They are also very good at their jobs and skillfully developed by their authors.

Characters We Love to Hate

Most series (books and TV) have characters we love and characters we'd like to strangle. Sometimes, it's the same person. Like *House*. I love it when he's painfully honest with an idiot who needs a dose of reality. I hate it when he's cruel to his boss and co-workers for no reason.

Then there's Ari Goldman on *Entourage*. (I can't believe I just admitted I watch this show.) He's horrible to everyone except his favorite client and his kids, but I still enjoy watching his character in action. I think it's the Jeremy Piven factor. I've been a fan forever. On the other hand, I simply loathe the Johnny Drama character on that show.

What about Dennis Leary's character in *Rescue Me*? He's a womanizer, an alcoholic, and an irresponsible lout. Few of the other men in his fireman crew are much better. Yet the show is strangely compelling.

Does an obnoxious/morally-challenged character make good entertainment?

Then there's Susan in the Spenser novels (Robert Parker). I quit reading this series long ago, but those who still love the series hate Spenser's girlfriend with an intensity. One mystery discussion participant posted, *Susan Silverman must die! Rarely has a more annoying character appeared in contemporary fiction.* Many mystery lovers say they quit reading the series because they hated her so much.

What is the difference between characters we love to hate and characters we simply hate (Ari Goldman versus Johnny Drama)? Are we more lenient with offensive male characters than offensive females?

I think most readers/TV watchers are attracted to extreme personalities, as long as the character has redeeming qualities, which can include simply being rich or smart. Being a hero, such as a doctor or firefighter, is even more redeeming.

Which characters do you love/hate? Which characters do you truly loathe? Have you ever quit a show or series because of a single character?

Character Descriptions

How do you feel about writers who don't describe their protagonists? How much description do you want to see?

I saw this question on a listserv today, and it hit home because I asked myself this same question yesterday. It occurred to me that there is almost no discussion of my protagonist's physical appearance in my new novel. In the first Detective Jackson mystery, readers get a brief description of Jackson from another main character early in the story. But in this installment, there is no opportunity for that. So anyone reading *Secrets to Die For* who did not read *The Sex Club* will have little idea what Jackson looks like—except that he's taller and heavier than a suspect who is coming at him.

I feel compelled to fix this. But there are limited options. He's not a man who will look in a mirror and assess his appearance. I may be able to sneak in little bits of physical information here and there, but it will not amount to a full description early in the story.

As readers, how do you feel about this? Are you okay with coming up with your own visualization? What happens when you picture a character as blond, blue-eyed, and stocky, only to learn 100 pages into the story that he's tall and dark? Is it disturbing, or do you just roll with the image?

Character Credibility

Neil Placky's excellent guest blog on The Kill Zone recently got me thinking about the nature of police proceduals. The series seem to fall into three camps: 1) protagonists who are always linked to the criminal case being solved, 2) cops who are sometimes linked to the case at hand, and 3) detectives who rarely have an emotional connection to the case they're working on. I'm not as widely read as I'd like to be, so my examples here are broad.

In the first category, the TV show *Murder She Wrote* comes to mind. In the third category, there's John Sandford's series about Lucas Davenport and Ridley

Pearson's series about Lou Boldt. Both detectives rarely have a personal stake in their cases' outcomes, yet they are favorites of mine—and millions of other readers.

My own series, and many others, falls somewhere in the middle. But even when Detective Jackson has a link to the case he's solving, it's not an intimate first-person connection.

I know many readers like emotional connections, but the question this raises for me is credibility. If the protagonist—whether a cop, FBI agent, reporter, or private detective—is surrounded by people who can't stay out of trouble, does he or she start to seem suspect? If every crime he or she solves is somehow personal, does your series start to lose credibility?

I left cozies out of the discussion because the personal connection theme seems inherent in the genre. And therefore, for some readers, cozies lack credibility. Shouldn't the standard also apply to more traditional crime/mystery novels?

I'm thinking about this now because I'm plotting my fourth Jackson story and wondering how important the personal connection is to readers.

Character History

This morning I wrote a scene in which my character thinks about his dead parents, and I had to stop and figure out whether I had mentioned in previous books what happened to them. It was real *duh* moment. My solution—to prevent readers from emailing me about character mistakes—is to go back and write a character development history. Then keep it updated as I go along.

I already have a character database in which I list every character who might possibly come up again, along with any pertinent details. But this project is specifically about Detective Jackson, his issues, his backstory, and his growth in each book. I should have done this from the beginning, but I wasn't sure with the first book that it would be a series. And I freely admit that plotting and pace are my strengths and character development is something I have to work harder at.

Keeping an ongoing history of Jackson's issues with his daughter, his ex-wife, his lover, his mysteriously dead parents—and his overall perspective—will help me with character development. It's also interesting to re-read the series back-to-back, with characterization in mind. The inconsistencies that jump off the page! The whole process is making me more aware of character, which is great for my writing.

A related issue is the risk of developing character story lines that continue through several books. What if an editor doesn't like the direction I've taken Jackson in the third book, which isn't published yet? What if she insists I take it out? Then much of the work I've done with Jackson in the fourth book will also have to be scrapped. So I'm being careful about what and how much I include. I'm also afraid to make the new character issues central to the plot

What is a Stereotypical Character, Anyway?

Recently someone posted on a listserv that he "wouldn't support an author who characterized all Irish people as ignorant and lazy or one who characterized all Jewish people as devious, greedy manipulators or one who painted all Sicilians as Mafiosi." That sounds reasonable on the surface, but it leaves me wondering: How does an author characterize ALL Irish people as ignorant and lazy? The presence of a single Irish character who happens to be lazy wouldn't give readers the idea that you were prejudiced against the Irish, would it? How many lazy Irish characters would you have to include in your novel for readers to come away with the idea that you had characterized ALL Irish people that way?

Or, for example, if you wrote a novel in which most of the characters were Sicilian and Mafioso (The Godfather), would readers assume the author thought ALL Sicilians were mob-connected? Does anyone think Mario Puzo is a racist?

Clearly, as novelists, we have to be careful about not playing into stereotypes. But stereotypes exist for a reason and are based on widely held perceptions. If you avoid every character detail that could be considered a stereotype, you'll end up with dull characters who don't resemble real people. To avoid offense, you could simply not label characters with any ethnic background. Still, you have to give everyone a name. Not having any ethnically associated names (O'Callahan, Schakowski, Botticelli) in your novel may go too far in the other direction and make you look like a WASP.

Then there's the popular TV show *Rescue Me.* The main character, Tommy Gavin, is Irish, alcoholic, and often out of control—and so is his whole family. The show plays directly into a stereotype. Are people offended by that? I'm certainly not. And I'm Irish and come from a family of alcoholics.

How do you portray real people with real ethnic backgrounds and flaws without offending readers or being labeled a bigot?

What's Wrong With Good Guys?

A post on Salon about detectives said most characters *...fail to capture our imaginations the way a gritty detective with a bad attitude and a drinking problem does.* It went on to say: *But even cops get boring after several decades of prime real estate on the small screen. That's why we need shows about time-traveling cops (Life on Mars), clairvoyant cops (The Mentalist, Medium), teenage detectives (Veronica Mars), obsessive-compulsive detectives (Monk), evil cops (The Shield), cops who work the system (The Wire) and many, many more.*

Does this premise apply to TV watchers only or has the need for quirky/morally-challenged/addicted cops taken over detective novels as well? Do cops have to have a *bad attitude and a drinking problem* or some other major character flaw to be interesting? What's wrong with a regular good guy/gal who has a clear understanding of what's right and wrong? A detective/FBI agent who is sober, thoughtful, and doing his/her best to balance work and family?

I say nothing is wrong with such a character. In fact, my recurring Detective Jackson is that person. He's not perfect, but his flaws are minor. If I had a daughter, I wouldn't worry if she got involved with him. That's not a bad test for whether your cop character is a good person: Would you want your daughter to date him? Would you be upset if your son married her?

Of course, there are the much-loved, loner-type Jack characters (Jack Reacher, Jack Taylor, etc.) who are fun to read, but in reality would cause sane women to run in the other direction.

Most of us read a mix of crime stories, from cozies to slasher/serial killers. Who are your favorite cop characters? Are they datable? Or are you attracted to those with *a drinking problem and a bad attitude*?

Chapter 5: All About Novels

The Power of K (12/08)

Marketers and comedians have long taken advantage of the powerful K sound. Crime writers have too, they just may not realize it. Think about the name Jack for protagonists. Jack Ryan, Jack Reacher, Jack Keller, Jack Taylor, Jack Davis, Jack Carpenter, Jack Irish, and Jack Palms to name just a few. Then there's Taylor Jackson and my own Detective Wade Jackson. Not to mention the Jakes (Jake Riley, Jake Riordan, Jake McRoyan).

The K sound is especially powerful at the end of word, which is why Jack and f**k are both so fun to say. Can you think of a comedian who can get through his/her material with saying f**k or jerk or some variation of jack (jackoff, jackass, jackshit)?

The X sound is really K with a little S on the end, so Alex is almost as popular with crime writers: Alex Cooper, Alex Cross, Alex Archer, Alex Delaware, Alex Duarte, Alex Bernier. And Cooper and Cross are both pronounced with the K sound. Then there's Kinsey Milhone and Greg McKenzie, which has a trifecta of winning sounds: the double K sound and the popular Z. Marketers like Z almost as well as K.

There's plenty of K sounds in other protags too: Lincoln Perry, Lucas Davenport, Elvis Cole, Kelly Jones, Joe Pike, John Cardinal, Michael Kowlaski, Vicky Bliss, and Jacqueline Kirby. My apologies to hundreds that I've likely missed.

In my recent novel, *The Sex Club*, which has both K and X sounds in the title, the main characters are Detective Jackson and Kera Kollmorgan. Jackson's daughter's name is Katie. In women's fiction, Kate is the female equivalent of Jack—a short, powerful K name (Kate London, plus many, many others).

It's not just me. Author Jack Getze has a protag named Austin Carr who encounters a bad guy named Max, whom he calls Creeper. In a single scene, he writes about Carr and Creeper as well as an AK-47, Alka-Seltzer, a stockbroker, an Escalade, a Caddy, and a Lincoln. Another writer told me, "I had so many K names in my first book I had to change all but one."

What is it about the K sound that we like so much? One amateur theory is that as babies, we all heard a lot of K words and noises: cootchie-coo, cutie-pie, cuddles, etc. But it could be that this is simply one of those things that is hard-wired into our brains from human experiences long ago. Whatever the reason, readers and writers like the sound K, so keep it coming.

What Makes Me Put Down a Novel (1/09)

I start many novels; I finish few. After years of writing, editing, and evaluating works of fiction, I have reader ADD. Here's what makes me put down a book:

- Slow start with too much day-in-the-life detail or too much backstory. I like it when a story makes me think *Oh shit* in the first few pages.
- Protagonists who do stupid things, especially before I start to like them.
- Stories that jump back and forth in time for no good reason
- Characters who have cutsie names or are obsessed with their pets. Sorry!
- Detailed gratuitous graphic violence.
- Detailed graphic sex scenes. They're all gratuitous unless you write erotica.
- Characters who bicker with their siblings or spouses. I've seen a lot of this lately.
- Too many characters introduced in the first few pages with no real explanation of who they are.
- Pages and pages with no dialogue.
- Protagonists who engage in immoral acts, like harming an innocent person. I need at least one person to root for.
- Long, meandering side stories that take me out of the main plot.
- Serial killers. No offense if you write them, I'm just burnt out.

Love It or Hate It? (1/09)

If I have learned one thing in these past few years of writing/publishing/reviewing, it is this: The reading experience is completely subjective. Of course, we've always known that some people like romance novels, while others read thrillers. But even within a genre such as mysteries, the opinions about a single novel vary greatly. As proof, year after year, the 4 Mystery Addicts listserv asks everyone to send in their top 10 reads of the year and their bottom 10 reads. Inevitably, several books make both lists.

This year, 17 books made at least one top and bottom list. Here are the five most loved/hated crime books (according to 4MA), with the first number in parenthesis representing how many top 10 lists it made, and the second number representing how many bottom 10 lists:

- The Girl With the Dragon Tattoo, Stieg Larsson (20, 3)
- Blue Heaven, C.J. Box (7, 2)
- Diamond Dove, Adrian Hyland (5, 1)
- Child 44, Tom Rob Smith, Tom (5, 1)
- The Various Haunts of Men, Susan Hill (4, 2)

Another mystery listserv, Dorothy L, also asks for best reads of the year, and oddly enough, there's very little overlap in the two groups' top 10 books, with the exception of *Blue Heaven* and *The Brass Verdict* by Michael Connelly.

It's also been interesting to observe reader discussions about Oprah's recent pick, *The Story of Edgar Sawtelle* by David Wroblewski. Some readers rave about it; others find it slow and tedious. Stephen King's *Duma Key* has generated even more conflicting reaction. My sense is that if you write something powerful, it will affect people both positively and negatively.

Have you ever read a book and loved it, then read it later and hated it?

What Makes Me Keep Reading (3/09)

I recently blogged about what makes me put down a novel, so to be fair, I thought I'd post about what makes me keep reading.

1. A great opening in which something unusual, unexpected, contradictory, or violent happens. For example, in *Secret Dead Men* by Duane Swierczynski, the third sentence caught my attention: *...but a couple of kids organized an impromptu club with a mandate to experiment on her corpse.*

2. Intriguing characters who are unusual, unexpected, contradictory, complex, or compelling. From the first page of the same story: *Then again, what do I know? I was a dead man impersonating an FBI agent.*

3. Characters who don't fit the current clichés. I like cops who aren't cynical, FBI agents who aren't workaholics that can't handle relationships, private investigators who aren't alcoholic loners, and women who are soft on the outside and tough on the inside.

4. **Complexity!** I like parallel plots, interwoven stories, and multiple points of view. And if it all comes together in a way that surprises me and makes perfect sense, I pick up the next book by that author.

5. Passion about a subject. I like politics, religion, and social issues in novels as long as it works for the story and doesn't overwhelm it.

6. Multiple plot points and plots twists that leave me thinking: Wow! Stunning, but believable.

7. Moderate levels of crime and violence written with sensitivity to the subject, the victim, and the reader.

8. Just enough detail (setting and character) to make the story real. I like Elmore Leonard's approach: Leave out the parts readers will skip.

9. Believable relationships of any and all kinds.

10. Fast-paced narrative with a great balance of dialogue and action, in which the surprises just keep coming.

Of course, these are the kind of stories I write too. ☺

First Name or Last? (6/09)

This question comes up dozens of times while I'm writing a novel. Almost every character is given two names (and sometimes a nickname), but what do you call them most consistently? First name or last? And does their gender and/or role in the story dictate which treatment they get?

I'm reading a John Sandford novel now (one of my favorite authors), and I noticed some patterns that made me wonder how other authors make these choices. There's a paragraph in which the mother and father of a murder victim are mentioned. Sandford refers to all of them by last name, Austin. It's quite confusing.

In later paragraphs—with the mother, who has the most prominent role of the three—Sandford rotates, sometimes calling her Allyssa and sometimes Austin. This was also confusing, because I'd only met her a few pages back. The author does this again later in a situation with a witness, calling her Brandt in one paragraph, then Jean in the next. I had to stop and figure out who he was talking about.

I suspect Sandford's novels may have always been like this, but I'm just now noticing because that writer/editor/evaluator part of my brain never shuts off anymore. I also notice that he calls his detective, Lucas Davenport, by his first name. Lucas' partners are Sloan and Del, and I honestly can't remember if they're first names or last.

As a novelist, to avoid confusion, my instinct in family situations is to call everyone by first name and have the detectives refer to them by first name or both. Even reporters do this in news stories for clarity. In my current novel, an entire family is victimized, and once their full names are established, I consistently refer to them by first name, with the last name added on as a reminder sometimes. I will likely continue that way throughout the rest of the manuscript.

My main character is Wade Jackson, but everyone calls him Jackson, including me, the narrator. And Jackson, a homicide detective, calls almost everyone he encounters—co-workers, suspects, and witnesses —by their last names. Only his daughter and girlfriend get first-name treatment. The young female victims in his cases get first-name treatment too.

The only time I go back and forth on a character's name is after that character (usually a suspect) is well established and I'm writing a scene, such as an interrogation, in which several males are consistently speaking. Using pronouns (he) in these situations is unacceptable, and I may call the suspect by his last name, Gorman, as general rule, then throw in Bruce every once in a while just to break things up.

I'm sure styles vary from genre to genre. In crime fiction—with cops, FBI agents, and private investigators as main characters—I think most co-workers, suspects and witnesses get the last name treatment, while family and friends get first names.

Readers: Do you have a preference? Do you like first names or last names better? Does it bother you when writers go back and forth and use different names for the same character?

The Politics of Sex and Crime (9/09)

What percentage of crime is rooted in sexual desire, frustration, deviancy, or possession? There are no stats for this broad spectrum, but according to the Bureau of Justice: *One third of female murder victims were killed by an intimate partner.* If you throw in abduction, assault by intimate partners, voyeurism, rape, and sexual abuse, it's easy to conclude that sexually motivated crimes are highly prevalent. But do they make good fiction?

According to an editor at a major publishing house, they're a tough sell. She says, "The sex crimes issues dealt with in both books remain topics that are very, very tough to make a success."

Can that possibly be true? How many bestsellers over the years have been about sexually motivated crimes? How many bestselling novelists (especially woman) consistently write about sex-based crimes? One unique example comes to mind. Chelsea Cain bases her police procedural/serial killer stories on a sexual attraction between the cop and the killer.

My novels are not based directly on sex crimes, but instead have the underlying theme of *sexual politics* as the motivation for the crimes. For me, that term covers a lot of ground: gender, sexual identity, sexual desire, sexual suppression, and reproduction. I believe these issues are the cornerstone of human behavior and form the basis (conscious or not) for many of our decisions.

In *The Sex Club*, the first story featuring Detective Jackson, I wrote about the repercussions of 1) teenage sex, 2) the suppression of sexuality, and 3) limited access to reproductive services. My primary goal though was (and continues to be) to tell a compelling story, and the novel has been extremely well received with hundreds of readers contacting me to say so.

In *Secrets to Die For*, another fast-paced police procedural, the events that unfold are rooted in the suppression of homosexuality and the violence that can spring from that. The book has just been released, and early readers are enthusiastic.

Thrilled to Death, the third Jackson novel, is a story about missing women, and on the surface doesn't seem to be about sexual politics. But in the long run, sexual deviancy is one of the motivations that sets events in actions.

The Baby Thief, a standalone thriller, explores the world of reproduction—women who want children (but not men in their lives) and women who want to have a child and can't... and the decisions they are driven to make.

This recurring theme is not intentional, but often when I explore connections between crimes that I see in the news, it seems to emerge. Sexual desire—and all its consequences—may be the most powerful motivator of human interactions. Money is a close second, and the story I'm writing now, *Passions of the Dead*, is more rooted in that *evil*.

Gender Matters (10/09)

Readers care much more about gender than I realized. Recent mystery forum discussions revealed some startling proclivities: Some women read only male writers. Other women often avoid female writers and protagonists because they fear they'll fit into certain stereotypes.

As a novelist, all of this concerns me. Especially considering four of the top five current fiction authors on the *New York Times* bestseller list are men, and that Oprah has picked 17 male authors and 2 female. I understand why men would read only male authors, but why do women make this choice? Do they believe men are intrinsically better writers? My father did. That's why I've always been published under L.J., even as a young journalist.

One thoughtful poster said: *I do consider gender when choosing books. I'm not a fan of chick-lit, cozies, or romancy 'women's' fiction. Nor am I a fan of crime fiction centered around feisty female protags with male-sounding names, bouncy red/ /blond/whatever hair, flashing green/blue /whatever eyes, and... well, you get the picture. Since all of the above are usually written by female authors, I find myself hesitating and investigating those authors (by visiting their website or reading more reviews, etc.) before committing to their books, while I tend to more readily give a male author's books a try without the vetting process.*

This honest viewpoint led me to examine my own preferences and book buying habits. I don't read chick-lit or cozies either, and I too avoid female characters who are bitter, overly smartass, or trying to prove themselves. As hard as this is to admit, I also think I subconsciously avoid new authors with feminine-sounding names (Stephanie, Ashley, Bethany). Now that I'm aware of it and why, I hope names and gender won't affect future book buying decisions.

Does that make you wonder if that's why I write a series about a male detective? The answer is no. In the first book—which didn't start out to be a series, it was just a story I had to tell—I had two main characters. The Planned Parenthood nurse had to be a woman, so I thought the detective needed to be a guy for balance. I also decided to write a cop I really liked in case I needed to bring him back in future books. I admit, now that I'm writing the series, I'm often glad Detective Jackson is a man. It would be harder for me to separate myself from a female protagonist and difficult to let a female character do things outside my comfort zone. It would also be nearly impossible for me to let a female protagonist make a mistake.

I'd be much more comfortable writing a female anti-hero, a character who starts out seriously flawed and develops over the course of a single, standalone story. Antagonists are a whole different scenario. Writing from their POV is like putting on a costume for a few hours at a time, with no long-term emotional association.

Book Discussion Questions (3/10)

Writing book-club discussion questions is one of those things writers put off and sometimes never get around to. But readers like them, so you might as well get it done. I've recently written my own, and it's not as tough as it seems. Here's some guidelines I put together to help you get started.

Ambiguity. If your novel leaves anything up in the air as to what really happened, this makes for a great discussion question. Readers love to determine the how and why of events that could go in different directions. *Did you believe the mayor's version of events? Why or why not? What do you think really happened?*

Motivation. Any question that gets to the heart of a character's motivation—especially to behave in a socially unacceptable way—will make for a lively discussion. *Jasmine shares privileged information with a reporter. Why? Claire says she stole the painting to protect it, but what were her real reasons?* I've discovered that readers bring their own experiences into a novel and often perceive things in characters that others don't, even the author. It's fascinating.

Fate. Questions that discuss the course of events and whether those events are inevitable will generate strong reactions from readers. *Did the young boy have to die in the end? Could the story have gone in another direction and still been effective?*

Coincidence. *Does the story rely on a major or minor coincidence? Was it believable and did it work for you? Was the story plausible overall?*

Values/beliefs. *In what ways do the events and characters reveal the author's values or world view? What is the author trying to say about* [insert hot-button issue here: women, race, sexuality, discrimination]? *Did the story make you question any of your own beliefs?*

What Readers Hate (1/11)

Always striving to improve my writing, I make notes when readers complain on forums about what they don't like in a story. I reviewed my notes recently because I'm working on a rewrite of a new novel. Here's a sample of *hates* from a mystery listserv I participate in:

- Portents, particularly the "had-I-but-known"
- Cliffhangers at the end of the chapter or the book
- An abundance of coincidences
- Too little character background for series protagonists, assuming the reader has read the previous books in the series
- Clumsy dialogue that doesn't sound natural
- Insufficient sense of place and/or time
- Characters that are TSTL (too stupid to live)

- Rushed endings, particularly done with exposition rather than actually solving the clues to solve the crime
- Abuse to women, children, or animals done for shock value
- A prologue that either isn't really necessary or that diminishes the impact later of the plot
- Characters with similar names
- Hackneyed plots
- Thin characters
- An unconvincing voice
- Weak, bland prose no matter what the style
- Pretentious prose no matter what the style
- Stylistic repetition that seems lazy
- Badly edited texts
- Deja vu: "I've read this before"
- The author trying too hard at whatever
- The author seeming to revel in cruelty

I'd like to think my stories don't fall into these patterns, but I confess, I occasionally use a cliffhanger at the end of a chapter, and my editor likes it.

Standalone Thrillers (4/11)

Readers are most familiar with my Detective Jackson books, but I also have two standalone thrillers I wrote before I started the series. I worked for a pharmaceutical magazine for years, so the books have subtle medical themes. I rewrote them last year to update the stories and to give Jackson a small cameo in each.

The seed of an idea that would become *The Baby Thief* sprouted one evening many years ago while I watched a few minutes of American Gladiator. I thought about how physically fit the winners were and how genetically superior their children would be. Eventually, I connected that idea to fertility science and the plot for *The Baby Thief* was born.

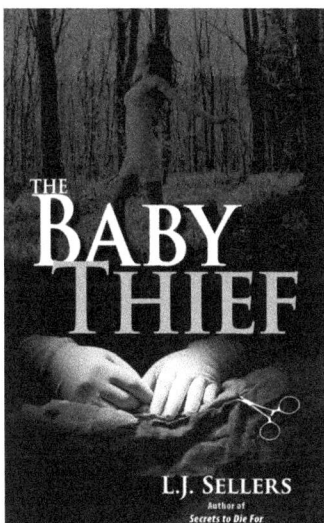

In essence, a woman goes to a fertility clinic, hoping to become artificially inseminated, but the clinic director takes one look at her and decides to steal one of her eggs to create a child of her own. Before that happens, the main character, Jenna, meets a charming reporter who won't let her disappearance go uninvestigated. Their relationship is a driving factor in the story, so I've recently labeled the book romantic suspense, and it's selling well on Kindle.

I wrote *The Suicide Effect* while working for the pharmaceutical magazine, and it reflects my concern that some antidepressant medication actually makes some people feel suicidal. The book's structure is similar to a woman-in-jeopardy novel, yet it's so much more than that. Sula, the protagonist, combats her deepest fears and risks everything to find the truth about the drug in question. Readers have said the ending made them shake in fear, then cry with joy. And for Jackson fans, he also makes a brief appearance. The Amazon reviews/ratings are terrific for both novels, and I hope you'll check them out.

I'm currently writing a third standalone thriller. This one features Detective Evans from my Jackson series, only it's set thirteen years in the future and she's no longer a cop. She's working as a freelance paramedic and getting ready to enter a national competition called the Gauntlet. Early in the story, she witnesses a crime, which later complicates her ability to compete. And then there's Paul, the federal software technician with access to personal data...

I'm excited about this story, which has a release date of September 7.

World Building: Less Is Better (8/11)

I'd wanted to write a futuristic thriller for years, but I knew it wouldn't be dystopian or fantasy-based. I imagined that the future world would be changed, and not for the better, but I didn't want it to be so different that it distracted from the story.

While writing *The Arranger*, I read a blog by a sci-fi author about world building, and it struck a chord with me. Essentially, the author said that world building is simply description and that description is boring. The author was making the point that readers want story—characters, events, and emotions—and that spending a lot of page time detailing the alternative world/future is counterproductive. A few brief, vivid sentences, or paragraphs, woven into the narrative are all you need to do the job.

I was relieved to be reminded of this facet of good writing. It saved me the trouble of creating a lot of unnecessary detail that a good editor would have made me cut or most readers would have skipped over.

Still, in the futuristic, sci-fi, and fantasy genres, readers expect a creative and unusual background, and I wanted to give them one. When I first started plotting this story, it never occurred to me that the backdrop would be an endurance competition called the Gauntlet. But characters often dictate the story, and once I decided that Lara Evans from my Jackson series would be the protagonist, I knew I had to give her an opportunity to be as physical as her character demanded. I also wanted to create a competitive environment for the unemployment crisis I foresaw in the future. From there, the Gauntlet was conceived.

Structuring and writing the competition scenes were the most challenging things I've ever done as a novelist.

For inspiration, I envisioned scenarios from American Gladiator, Wipe Out, and a little Fear Factor thrown in, but I stepped up the intensity and duration and pushed the contestants right to the edge. I also gave the worldwide viewers the ability to alter the contest—to reward or punish contestants with the level of difficulty. That created some surprising moments for the contestants.

It was important to me that the competition had at least one intellectual component, so that the overall contest couldn't be won by sheer strength or endurance. So I created the Puzzle, a locked-room situation that requires a MacGyver-type solution, with timing counting toward a win. The brainteaser seemed particularly important because in the Gauntlet, men and women compete against each other. Don't worry, ladies, my protagonist kicks ass.

The contest is only one element of the plot though. There's also a parallel story told by Paul Madsen, a software technician who's given access to information that he can't resist exploiting. In Paul's world, the federal government is a fraction of its former size and is a lean, mean employer. But again, I made a conscious choice not to bog down the story with extraneous detail about bureaucratic structure.

Admittedly, Lara's world was more fun to write about, but Paul's world is the one I fear could come to pass. I hope readers enjoy both scenarios and find the level of detail I've included to be just right.

Chapter 6: Writing and Editing Advice

My Writing Process

For some novelists, the act of writing is a mystic, free-flowing, almost out-of-body experience. Then there are people like me who approach it with a collection of notes, databases, and timelines—a process almost as pedantic as end-of-year bookkeeping. But in my defense, I must point out that I create complex crime stories that come together without any gaping holes. So if you lean toward compulsive and would like to know how I do this, here's my process:

1. Create an outline. Once I have a basic story idea—comprised of an exciting incident, major plot developments, and overview ending—I start filling in the details. I structure my outline by days (Tues., Wed., etc.), then outline the basic events/scenes that happen on each day, noting which POV the section will be told from. For police procedurals (and most mysteries), in which everything happens in a very short period of time, this seems essential. Some people (like Stephen King) will tell you not to outline, that it ruins creativity. I respectfully disagree. So I fill in as much detail as I can at this point, especially for the first ten chapters and/or plot developments. For the record, I don't have the entire story mapped at this point. And I used Word or Excel for all my files. (*Current update: I've started using Scrivener, and I love it.*)

2. Create a list of POV characters. I also generate a brief personality sketch and physical description for them. Some of my main characters are recurring, so the information already exists, but there's an opportunity here to make changes if you want your characters to age, lose weight, or color their hair. My rule is never more than five POV characters telling the story, and some characters (bad guys and victims) have only small POV roles. Eventually, I'll add these characters and their information to my major database of characters. (See # 9.)

3. Begin writing. I don't worry about crafting perfect opening lines at this point. I simply start writing a scene, because that's the only way I know to get a story moving. I've been fortunate in coming up with opening lines that work well and need little revising.

4. Beef up the outline. As I write the first 50 pages or so, new ideas come to me and I fill in the rest of the outline as I go along. I continue adding to the outline, and by about the middle of the story, I have it completed.

5. Create a timeline. A lot happens in my stories, which usually take place in about six to ten days. I keep the timeline filled in as I write the story. This way I can always look at my timeline and know exactly when an important event took place (*Monday, 8 a.m.: Jackson interrogates Gorman in the jail*). It's much faster to check the timeline than scroll through a 350-page Word document. The timeline also keeps me from writing an impossible number of events into a realistic day.

6. Keep an idea/problem journal. I constantly get ideas for other parts of the story or realize things I need to change, so I enter these notes into a Word file as I think of them. *Ryan needs to see Lexa earlier in the story, where?* I keep this file open as I write. Some of these ideas never get used, but some prove to be crucial. Eventually, all the problems get resolved as well. I now use the Notebook layout feature in Word for this, so I can keep the outline, timeline, notes, problems, and evidence all in the same file, using different tabs. I love this feature.

7. Keep an evidence file. This idea won't apply to romance novels, but for crime stories, it's useful. I make note of every piece of evidence that I introduce and every idea I get for evidence that I want to introduce. I refer to this file regularly as I write, so that I'm sure to process and/or explain all the evidence before the story ends. In my first novel, *The Sex Club*, a pair of orange panties didn't make it into the file or the wrap up, and sure enough, a book club discussion leader asked me who they belonged to.

8. Update my character database. It took me a few stories to finally put all my character information into one database, but it was a worthwhile effort. Now, as I write, I enter each character name (even throwaway people who never come up again) into the database, including their function, any physical description, or any other information such as phone number, address, type of car, or favorite music. Now, when I need to know what I named someone earlier in the story or in a previous novel, it's right there in my Excel database (*Zeke Palmers; morgue assistant; short, with gray ponytail*). For information about how to set up a file like this, see the next post.

9. Stop after 50 pages. As a general rule, I like to get the whole story down on the page before I do much rewriting, but I've learned to stop at this point for two reasons. One, I like to go back and polish the first chunk of the story in case an agent or editor asks to see it. Two, I usually give this first chunk to a few beta readers to see if I'm on the right track.

10. Use the highlight feature. If I'm on a roll with a particular scene but don't know a street name or the exact spelling of something, I'll tag it with yellow highlight and keep going. Of course I come back to everything eventually, but why let these details interfere with the flow of writing?

11. Rewrite. In the second draft, I constantly refer to my evidence file and my idea/problem file to ensure that every issue is dealt with. I delete the items as I process them in the story. My first draft is usually lean, with mostly dialog and action, so in the second draft, I fill in details for scenery and characterization, add some scenes, and slow the story down in places. I never add too much description, of course. I'm a big fan of Elmore Leonard, who says to leave out all the stuff that people don't read anyway.

How to Create a Character Database

I recently set up a character database in Excel, and when I posted the update on Twitter and Facebook, several people contacted me and asked, *What's a character database?* Sensing that this subject might be interesting to others, I decided to share the details. First, let me say that I'm not an Excel whiz kid, so trust me when I say this file set up is really straightforward.

This type of database is especially useful if you write a series, and I finally set it up because I got tired of having to look back to see how I had described a character in a previous novel or search endlessly for the name of a street. I started the file in a Word document, but it was too messy and didn't allow nifty sorting features.

First, I established the column headers across the top. I'm still tweaking as I go, but for now I have:

- First name
- Last name
- Category
- Role/Function
- Description
- Car, Address, Phone
- Other Details
- Book title 1 (The Sex Club)
- Book title 2 (Secrets to Die For)
- Book title 3 (Thrilled to Death)
- Book title 4 (The Baby Thief)

Most of these headers are self-explanatory, but the Category column is where I assign the character's level: 1=main character/recurring, 2=main character/specific to novel, 3=villain, 4=secondary character/recurring, 5=throwaway characters.

Next, I listed the characters by row and inserted relevant information. I still have to go back into *The Sex Club* and find/input all the secondary characters, but with this novel, I'm adding to the database every time I add important details to the manuscript.

What's great about this file is that each column can be sorted individually. I separated out the first and last names so I could alphabetize/sort each list individually. So if I come up with the name Kirstin, I can quickly sort first names and check the middle of that column and see how many characters have first names that start with K. Yikes! Better come up with a different name.

The purpose of the book title columns is to be able to sort by title. I simply put an X in each column title that the character is present in. Then if I'm working in Book #3, I can sort by that column and have all the Book #3 characters come to the top of the spreadsheet, allowing me easy access to their information. And if I have one of those moments when I'm wondering—*Was Officer Chang in my first story or just my second?*— it's easy to find out.

Important reminder: Even if you're sorting by a single column, be sure to highlight all your data so the information for each row/character stays together. I hope you find this idea useful...and comprehensible.

Story Logic—Spell It Out

For the last two days, I've been filling in the details of my outline, working out the timeline, and crafting a sizzling ending that brings my new story all together. I'm already 80 pages into writing my fifth Detective Jackson story, and it was time to solidify some plot points. I know many writers (Stephen King, for example) don't do this; they prefer to wing it and see where the story takes them.

But I write a mystery/suspense series with complex plots, overlapping stories, and critical timelines. I've never felt like I had the luxury of winging it. So I produce detailed outlines as well as current and past timelines. But I take the planning process a step further, and it may be the most important thing I do for every novel.

In a police procedural, so much happens in the first few days of a murder investigation that a timeline is essential. For complex, parallel plots with multiple points of view, mapping the story in detail is the best way to avoid writing myself into a dead end or writing 48 hours worth of activity into a 10-hour timeframe. I speak from experience.

Then yesterday for the first time, I put in writing what I termed *story logic*. I've always done this in my head to some degree, but this was the first time I put it on the page in summary form. In a mystery/suspense novel, some or much of what happens before and during the story timeline is off the page—actions by the perpetrators that the detective and reader learn of after the fact. Many of these events and/or motives are not revealed until the end of the story. I was worried that I wouldn't be able to convey to readers how and why it all happened.

So I mapped it out—all the connections, events, and motivations that take place on and off the page. *Bad guy Bob knows bad guy Ray from prison. Bob meets young girl at homeless shelter. Young girl tells Bob about the money she found . . .*

It was an enlightening process, and I highly recommend it. Summarizing the story logic forces you to think specifically about character connections and motivations. It points out holes and inconsistencies and gives you an opportunity to tighten and improve your plot. It may even force you to rethink and rewrite your outline. But it also may keep readers from getting to the end of your novel and thinking, *How did he know that? Where did that come from?*

I mentioned the process on a Twitter/Facebook update, and another writer asked me about it. So I explained it to her (in 140 characters!). She got back to me with this message: "I wrote the foundation of my book and did the 'story logic' for the rest before writing the book to fill in details. It led me in a completely different direction. I took some risks in the outline and a lot fell into place. I'm psyched!"

I admit, all of this takes some of the spontaneity out of the writing process. But for me, writing isn't magic. It's work, and it needs the same detailed planning as any other project. Of course, I'm flexible. If better ideas or connections come to me as I write, I will modify my outline and re-summarize the story logic.

10 Steps to a Better Story

I've edited and evaluated a lot of fiction, and I see a pattern of common problems in manuscripts from novice writers. The most important involve the bond between story and character. If you want an agent or editor to get past the first page, here's 10 things to keep in mind.

1. Make your main character want something. Desire is the engine that drives both life and narrative. Characters who don't want anything are rarely interesting.

2. Make your main character do something. Your story can start with a character who is the victim of circumstances, but afterward, the character needs to move quickly into action. Readers like characters who take charge.

3. Let your readers know the story's premise early. If they get to the end of the first chapter and still can't answer the question—*What is the story about?*—they might not keep reading.

4. Get conflict into the story early. It doesn't have to be all-out bickering or deception between characters, but let your readers know things will get sticky.

5. Skip the omniscient POV. Let the reader experience as much of the story as possible through the eyes of your main character. This is how readers bond with protagonists. If you shift perspective, at least put in a line break.

6. It's okay to tell sometimes, instead of show. Not every character reaction has to be described in gut-churning, eyebrow-lifting, physical detail. Sometimes it's okay to simply say, "Jessie panicked."

7. Introduce characters one at a time with a little background information for each. Too many characters all at once in the first few pages can be overwhelming.

8. Don't over write. Nobody agrees on what constitutes good writing, so trying to make your writing stand out will probably work against you. The best writing doesn't draw attention to itself; it just gets out of the way of the story.

9. Avoid word repetitions when you can. Read your story out loud. You're much more likely to hear the repetitions than see them.

10. The components of a novel that readers care about most are, in order: **story, characters, theme, and setting**. If you have to sacrifice something, start at the end of the list. Never sacrifice the story for anything else.

Publisher Evaluations

I used to evaluate fiction manuscripts for a publisher, using a standard form crafted by the publishing house. The form contained a list of questions, grouped by subject: premise, plot, POV, character, dialogue, and setting. I'm sharing some of the questions so you can see specifically how a publisher might evaluate your manuscript.

Opening:
- Does the first page grab the reader's attention?
- Does the first chapter set up the basis for the rest of the story?

Premise and Tone:
- Is the basic premise or theme interesting? Believable? Unique?
- Is the focus of the work revealed early in the novel?
- Is the basic premise of the novel well executed?

Point of View:
- Is the point of view consistent throughout?
- Are shifts in point of view, if any, necessary and simple to follow?
- Is the point of view used appropriately to convey the thoughts or emotions of various characters?

Structure, Plot, and Pace:
- Is there a planned series of carefully selected interrelated incidents?
- Are there situations that heighten the conflict?
- Does the story have a clear conclusion or satisfactory ending appropriate to the genre?
- Do the plot and structure sufficiently hold the reader's interest throughout?

Setting:
- Is the setting described appropriately without slowing the pace of the work?
- Does the novel provide an appropriate sense of place?

Characterization:
- Does the author provide a clear visual image of the characters?
- Does the behavior of all characters seem realistic?
- Are the characters presented with realistic challenges and life situations?
- Do you feel an emotional connection to any of the characters?
- Are characters introduced effectively and for a specific purpose?

Dialogue:
- Does the dialogue reveal the character's background or identifying traits?
- Is there a good balance of dialogue and action?

- Does the dialogue sound authentic, and is it used effectively throughout?

Advice From a Reader

A prolific reader and book reviewer posted this list of personal tips in a discussion forum. If you're working on a novel, it's worth a read, but it's also just one reader's opinion, and I don't necessarily agree with everything.

1. Don't give me time shifts or reverse time chapters unless you clearly indicate what you are doing and the purpose is absolutely necessary to make your story work.

2. No backstory after chapter one. If it's that important, you should have written the earlier book instead. *(Author's current note: Some backstory not revealed until late in the story can build suspense.)*

3. Don't assume I have read all your previous books, but don't fully include them in the current book unless relevant.

4. Refrain from obscure references outside the current book. No, I don't recall what painting is hanging on the far west wall in the room of the Louvre just beyond where the Mona Lisa is displayed, and frankly, my dear, I don't give a damn.

5. Give your characters names that make sense but stay away from cutesy and/or tongue twisters that no one will remember. Also if your female characters are all Sue, Sue Anne, Suzanne, Susie, Susan, and all your males are Mike, Michael, Mikie and Mikhiel, well, forget it.

6. Check your facts. You don't have to be perfect, but please no ballistic checks for rifling on shotguns (there aren't any), no Chevrolet Thunderbirds, etc. The basics should always be right.

7. You can take certain liberties with reality if it makes story sense. It's much better to have a temporary suspension of belief than an overly convoluted plot sequence just to make it work.

8. Limit coincidences. Yes, they do occur. But how often have you been walking down the street in a strange city, stop to help a little old lady cross the street, and discover she is your ex-wife's fourth grade school teacher?

9. Don't be unkind to animals or kids. I will throw your book against the wall whenever you beat, hit, kick, burn, or otherwise abuse either. Yes, there are animal abusers and child abusers in the real world, but not in mine.

10. Stereotypes are usually okay. After all, they help us quickly picture a character based on our real-life experiences. On the other hand, what I call an anti-stereotype can be distracting, i.e., if you paint the character one way and then have him/her act out of character.

Reader Requests

I recently asked readers in a Kindle forum what they would like to see more of in novels. Here are the answers, verbatim.

- Mysteries in which you are given sufficient clues to figure it out before the detective does.
- Humor applied like seasoning throughout the book, in narration and dialog, and of a dry or tongue-in-cheek nature.
- Underdogs.
- Romances that develop unpredictably, with all the illogical surprises real ones have.
- Rivals who develop respect for each other and possibly even become friends.
- Themes of brotherhood.
- A devil-may-care protagonist who doesn't get depressed (like I do) when life dumps tons of manure on them.
- An author who knows what he/she is writing about, and can effortlessly, comfortably "speak

the language" of people from the subculture they depict.

- Fantasy authors who keep made-up, foreign-sounding words to a minimum.
- Breaking of current conventions (but not just for the sake of breaking conventions).
- Climaxes that live up to the hype/buildup.
- Science fiction that focuses more on character than technology. (Technology is a prop, or backdrop.)
- Characters who make mistakes, but not as many as I do.
- Clean prose without consistent amateurish blemishes.
- New plot developments that force me to radically reinterpret everything I read before!

Checklist for Your Novel

Story arc: Does the protagonist grow and evolve? Is the narrative smooth or does it have gaps in logic?

Plot: Is your plot logical? Do you have important scenes that would make a reader think, *No one would ever do that*? Is your plot both linear and complex?

Point of view: Is your POV consistent for large chunks of text? Do you tell each scene from the point of view of the character who has the most to lose?

Dialogue: Does each character use distinctive word choices? Do you break up long conversations with body language and movement?

Info dumps: Do you have big chunks of exposition that slow down the story? Can they be broken up or shared as dialogue?

Characters: Are your characters both believable and unique? Is their behavior consistent within the story framework?

Language: Do you use of mix of long and short sentences? Are there overused words or phrases (of course, just, even, that)?

Unresolved issues: Is every plot line resolved and questions accounted for? If something is bothering you, it will bother your readers.

Great Story Starts

The evaluation form I complete for a publisher asks: Is the focus of the novel revealed early? Most of the time, I check *Needs Work*. Writers often move slowly in the beginning, setting up backstory or crafting beautiful irrelevant scenes. Two chapters later, I still don't know what the premise is. The best stories jump right in and reveal what the character wants and/or what the character is up against to get what he wants.

Revealing the focus can be indirect. In a coming-of-age story I just evaluated, the first page opens with a mother having a confrontation with a customs inspector, as seen through her daughter's eyes. It was clear the story would be about the daughter's confrontations with her mother and her struggle to become independent. The scene was also filled with tension and showed the mother's character. I was captivated—and I don't usually read coming-of-age stories.

Start your story in the middle of a situation. Write a scene with dialogue, action, conflict, and/or yearning. Let the reader know what your story is about. You can always go back later and fill in.

Writing Tips From an Editor

I'm fine-tuning the novel I just finished, and these are some edits I'm making. They can help you as you write or edit your own novel.

Get rid of unnecessary prepositional phrases. When you read back through your manuscript, watch for phrases like *on the table*, *toward the door*, *near the* *wall.* These phrases bog down your writing and often add little to a description. Readers can make a lot of assumptions. If two guys are standing in the driveway talking and one points at the tires, readers will assume you mean *on the car.* You don't have to say it.

This is especially true at the end of sentences. A good sentence ends on a strong beat. The previous sentence is a great example of what I mean. If I had added the word *usually* at the end, it would have weakened the sentence. In my manuscript, I came across this sentence: *Katie put her waffle down on the paper in her lap.* Ick!

I took off the first unnecessary phrase, then the second. Then I moved the word *down* to where it belongs—after the verb directing it. Now it reads: *Katie put down her waffle.* Much better! Nobody cares where the waffle went. The sentence is meant to show that what Katie is about to say next is so important she wants no distractions.

Get rid of unnecessary pronouns. Here's how a sentence in this blog read until I edited it: If two guys are standing in the driveway talking and one of them points at the tires, readers will assume you mean on the car. I took out *of them.* Readers know I meant the two guys, and the sentence reads better without the phrase. Other examples are phrases like *himself* or *to me.* Often you'll discover they are unnecessary.

Be careful in using pronouns. I've gotten much better about this over the years, thanks to Stephen King's *On Writing*, but I still see the problem in the fiction manuscripts I edit for others. In a confrontation scene with three guys, for example, the writer will use *he* and *his* repeatedly. It's very confusing. In these situations, be redundant, regardless of whose POV you're writing from. Use each man's name every time you refer to him. Readers will appreciate it.

Jake picked up the gun and aimed it at Seth. Seth ran for the door, while Carl yelled, "Don't do this." Jake lowered the gun. Carl lunged at a Jake. Seth kept running.

Even a single use of *he* in that paragraph could have made it hard to follow.

Style It Right

As a fiction editor, I encounter confusion from writers about how to treat numbers, the time of day, and references to printed materials. I base my edits/suggestions on a combination of *Chicago Manual of Style* and what I see and experience from traditional publishers. As a submitting novelist, you might as well get your manuscript into the best shape you can before sending it to anyone.

Here are some general guidelines:

1. Numbers one through one hundred are usually spelled out as words. Larger numbers, especially dollar amounts, can be written as numerals, especially if it's more readable. Be consistent within a paragraph. Examples:

- Lucy had seen the movie twelve times and spent exactly $132.45 in the process.
- At age ninety-nine, Stella always let her cats out when she left the house.
- Still, she hoped to make it to a hundred and two, just to show up her sister.

2. If you give an exact time of day, use numerals and lowercase for a.m. and p.m. Few publishers use small caps anymore. For general hour references, which could have *o'clock* after them, use words. Examples:

- Jackson looked at his watch: 1:45 p.m.
- He'd gotten up that morning at four and left the house by five.

3. Use numerals for years, but never use an apostrophe. Decades aren't possessive. Example:

- She left home in 1982 but didn't mature until she took up meditation in the 90s.

4. Gun calibers should be expressed in numerals, even in dialogue. Examples:

- Granny loaded her Ruger .22 and took aim.
- "I'll get the Colt .45," Gramps shouted.

5. Almost all references to printed materials can be made italic. Quote marks should be reserved for spoken dialogue in novels. Examples:

- Janie used her copy of *Rolling Stone* to fan away the smoke.
- In a moment of clarity, she grabbed a pen and wrote out a list: *get a job, lose five pounds, call my mother.*

Internal Dialogue: First Person or Not?

Recently an editor at a small publishing house wanted me to rewrite all internal dialogue in first person, present tense. My novel is written in third person, past tense. She said first person is standard for internal dialogue, and she also urged me in several places to change the text to internal dialogue. I didn't do it.

As a reader, if I'm reading a third-person, past-tense story and suddenly the author switches to first person, present for internal dialogue, I find it jarring.

So I don't write internal thoughts that way. I try to keep the internal dialogue to a minimum, because the formatting requires italics, and so many readers hate italics. "Distracting, annoying, and hard to read," they say. So my internal dialogue is often quite brief, a word or phrase. Even when it's longer, it stays in third person.

The first example following is how I wrote it. The second example is how the editor wanted to change it to first person and italics.

1. Conner hit the floor and did forty push-ups, muscles responding as they were trained to. The effort calmed him enough to sit down and continue his search of the paperwork. He willed himself to be cool and logical. **First, find the address, then go get Bodehammer.**

2. Conner hit the floor and did forty push-ups, muscles responding as they were trained to. The effort calmed him enough to sit down and continue his search of the paperwork. He willed himself to be cool and logical. **First, I'll find the address. Next I'll go get Bodehammer.** I polled my Twitter and Facebook followers and they said it was better my way, so I didn't make the change. *(Author's current note: I just had a reader contact me and say my latest story, The Arranger, would have been better with more first-person internal dialogue. Clearly, you can't please everyone.)*

The style and level of internal dialogue may vary between genres, but in the crime stories I read, I couldn't find any examples of first person internal dialogue in third person narratives. In fact, there was hardly any internal dialogue or italics at all.

Self-Editing Tips

Get rid of the word *that*. In my last writing-tip blog, I originally wrote this sentence: If two guys are standing in the driveway talking and one points at the tires, readers will assume that you mean on the car. I went back and took out *that*. The sentence reads better without it. You'll see this is true most of the time you use *that*. Every once in a while the word will be needed for clarity but not often.

Get rid of verbs that end in *ing*. Of course, they're necessary sometimes, but *ing* verbs are weak. Use present or past tense verbs as much as possible. *Jackson ran for the door* is stronger than *Jackson was running for the door*.

Get rid of *it*. When rewriting, I replace this pronoun at least half the time with the name of the thing it represents. In verbal communication, repetitive use of *it* may be acceptable, but in narrative writing, such lack of clarity is ineffective and often confusing.

Resist starting sentences with *But, And*, or *Then*. We'll all do it when we're in writing mode and the point is to crank out a scene and get words on the page without worrying about finesse. In rewrite mode, I use the search function to locate these words when they're capped and eliminate them as sentence starters as much as possible. But I make exceptions.

Use the search function to find errors. When I notice I've misspelled a character's name, I assume I've done it more than once, so I search for the misspelled version. If I see I've treated a phrase in different ways, say, hyphenated in one use and open in another, I search for it both ways and standardize my usage.

Tweak individual scenes so they read like mini-stories, with mounting tension, a climax, and a conclusion. The exceptions to that structure are scenes at the end of chapters, which I often leave with a revelation, a hint of a revelation, or some uncertainty (aka, cliffhangers).

Common Word Misuse

When you work with the same group of editors for a long time, it becomes a training ground in which you learn to accommodate each other's styles—especially those of the editor-in-chief. If the big boss hates the word *impact* (except when talking about car accidents), then everyone learns to edit the word out of their own writing and out of the articles they're editing. I worked on the same magazine for seven years, and both bosses were fond of *The Careful Writer* by Theodore Bernstein. So I learned not to misuse certain common words, and now I make these edits consistently in the documents of my main client. In turn, the writers at this company are now self-correcting these mistakes. Here are a few of the most common word usage errors:

Since is a time reference and should not be used to imply cause. Many people had it drilled into their heads that they can't start a sentence with *because*, so they write: *Since delegation is the only way to get things done, I now....* It is more correct to write: *Because delegation is the only way ....*

The word *over* is meant to describe a location. She drove over the bridge. The book is over there. So the statement, *Over six thousand people attended the event,* would be better written as, *More than six thousand.* I know. Everybody says *over*, even TV newscasters who make a lot of money. It's still correct to say *more than.* Here's another common misusage of this word: We reached a milestone over the past year. Correct usage calls for: We reached a milestone *during* the past year. If you're writing nonfiction, why not be as precise as possible?

The word *while* is also a time reference: You go out and play, while I stay here and clean. Yet many people use *while* to start a sentence to refute something: While it's usually a good idea to start early, in this case, we'll wait. That sentence is better constructed with although. *Although* it's usually a good idea…

On is also meant to describe location: The book is on the desk. One of the most irritating phrases I see again and again is *information on.* For more information on this subject, go to our website. Nope. It should be: For more information *about* this subject . . .

The Careful Writer is a great resource even if the author is a little snooty. For the record, I agree with him about the word *impact.* Never use it as a verb, and the word *impacted* should refer only to wisdom teeth or dysfunctional bowels.

New Rules for Writers

Most of these are actually old rules, but these offenses have popped up repeatedly in documents I've edited, so they're worth dusting off and revisiting.

1. Avoid using buzzwords, especially in a way in which they were not originally intended. Examples include: impact, utilize, incentivize. *Impact* used to be a noun that referred to the effect of a collision; *utilize* means "to find a profitable or practical use for," and *incentivize* just makes me shudder. *Affect*, *use*, and *motivate* are more reader friendly and easier to spell.

2. Don't fill your novel (or report) with clichés. Hanging by a thread, cold as ice, dead as a doornail (whatever the hell that means) are old hat and old school. You can be more creative.

3. Why use *ing* verbs when present tense verbs work harder?
- Soggy: She was jogging down the sidewalk when a car suddenly started veering off the road...
- Crisp: She jogged down the sidewalk. Suddenly, a car veered off the road ...

4. Keep verbs phases together whenever possible.
- Acceptable: She *dropped* Micah *off* and *picked* the book *up*.

- Better: She *dropped off* Micah and *picked up* the book.

5. If you're writing a novel, do not have adult siblings bicker like children. It is not entertaining. Really!

6. Introduce characters one at a time, please. If you throw too many at the reader all at once, none will stick.

7. Don't give your characters sound-alike names such as Dan, Dave, and Dean, even if they are brothers or psychic twins. Help your readers keep everyone straight with names like Moon Unit, Dweezil, and Ahmet. Kidding! Those are Frank Zappa's kids' names. But you get my point.

The Curse of Commas

Commas are the single worst thing about being an editor. How can such a tiny little piece of punctuation cause so much time-sucking anguish? The rules are both inflexible and squishy at the same time.

Rule One: Two independent clauses separated by a conjunction need a comma. So the following sentence (with two subjects: he and it) is punctuated correctly with a comma. He started the car, and it made a noise.

This next sentence (with only one subject: he) is also punctuated correctly without a comma. He started the car and drove around town for a few hours but soon got bored and went home to clean out the garage and mow the lawn.

This drives writers crazy because these examples make no visual or auditory sense. Nobody wants a comma in the first example, and everybody wants to put a comma between *hours* and *but* in the second example.

Here's the squishy part. Technically, the comma in the second example isn't necessary, but many editors and publishers allow authors some discretion in using commas to direct the reader to pause. So you'll see it both ways.

Here's more squish. Nonfiction writing is more formal and requires closer adherence to the rules, while in fiction the style is more open. This means in novels, rule number one is frequently ignored. But every book publisher has its own in-house rules, and every newspaper or magazine has its own style. No wonder most writers have given up trying to get commas right.

Not to mention the introductory clauses, for which the punctuation is completely discretionary. In an academic paper, you'll see a comma after even the shortest introductory phrases/words: In time, the relationship between the two variables...

In fiction, you'll see no common after long and complex introductory phrases: On the morning after the big explosion in the airport hanger he packed his suitcase and headed...

Where is the logic? As an editor and writer, I try to follow the rules and consider the genre, but I also try to be logical and fair to the reader. My priority is always readability first, grammar rules second.

Enough With the Scare Quotes

Quote marks are the most overused form of punctuation. *Quote* is short for *quotation*, so essentially, quote marks should be used only to set off a quotation—the verbatim text of something that was said or published. If you're writing a novel and using quote marks for anything but dialogue—take them out.

Writers everywhere like to use quote marks around words they consider special for some reason or around words that are not being used in a traditional way. Old school editors call them *scare quotes*, a way of alerting the reader that the word isn't being used in a traditional way. Ninety percent of the time, the marks are completely unnecessary. If you're writing logical sentences, readers know what you mean. Here are a few examples of unneeded scare quotes.

"Quote" is short for "quotation." Did anyone misread the sentence when I wrote it earlier with just italic?

After a few minutes in the club, John decided to wander back and watch the "dancers." Yes, we all know *dancers* is a polite way of saying strippers. Does your character think of them as dancers or strippers? Use one or the other, without quote marks, because it tells us something about your character.

Many editors will argue that in my first example, quote marks are necessary to set off the words used as words. (Oh, the many discussions I've had about words as words!) The true test is readability. If the sentence reads fine without the punctuation, don't use it. Less is better. If you have to set off the word used as a word for readability, use italic, which is less intrusive, and *Chicago Manual of Style* says is preferable.

For a look at some extremes of excessive quote mark usage, check this site. The Blog of Unnecessary Quotation Marks: http://quotation-marks.blogspot.com.

When to Ignore Good Advice

Advice for writers is everywhere. Rules for writing. Rules for querying. Rules for submitting. I also actively solicit advice from writers, readers, agents, and others in the publishing business. There have been times when I followed what seemed like good advice and ended up regretting it. Other times, I ignored what seemed like good advice and was glad I did. How do you know up front when to ignore sound advice? Listen to your own instincts.

For example, an agent one advised me to write a young adult (YA) novel because she knew an editor who was looking for YA manuscripts that dealt with dark, real-life scenarios, and she thought I would be perfect for the series. My instinct said it wasn't right for me, but

I thought the agent had a solid connection that would get me published. A total waste of time! I am not a YA writer. I'm not sure I was every really young. My mother swears I was born 40.

One very successful agent who I signed with kept advising me to write a cozy mystery series because "that's what all the publishers wanted." I don't read cozy mysteries, and I didn't think I could pull it off. So I never tried. That was smart. See above. So my rule for myself is: Never write a novel you wouldn't read.

A beta reader once advised me to not make the murder victim's mother a drug addict who had died of drug-related complications. She thought it was distracting and unnecessary. Yet it was the basis for the character's personality. It was why she ended up in the situation she was in at the time of the murder. Wrong advice! Easy to ignore.

Everyone in the business says to never query an agent before you finish writing the story. I routinely ignore this advice (when sending snail mail), and I have never had an agent respond to a query before the manuscript was ready. Agents are notoriously slow—I once got a response three years and three months later—so why not eliminate the waiting gap with writing time? Sending queries early also motivates me to get the novel done.

A successful mystery writer and dear friend once advised me not to approach an editor at a major publishing house directly. She felt strongly that I should get an agent, because the editor would never consider a manuscript submitted without one. But this editor had read *The Sex Club* and loved it. She knew my name and my writing, so I felt there was no harm in asking if she'd like to see the next installment in the Jackson series. So I queried her directly anyway. Then I met her in person at Bouchercon and pitched the novel again. A month later, she emailed me and asked to see the manuscript. I'm still waiting to see how it turns out, but even if she passes, I'm still glad I ignored that professional advice and followed my instinct.

I have learned to write only the stories I feel passionately about, regardless of what's currently trendy. I've also learned to trust my own instincts about what works best for those stories. Of course, you are free to ignore any advice I might give you.

New Writing Resolutions

1. Write every day. That means during the week, spend a minimum of three hours on my current big project and on weekends, write blogs, articles, short stories, comedy material, letters to the editor—almost anything to keep the juices flowing.

2. Write bold. Do not be afraid to offend an occasional reader. I can't make everyone happy. If I did, my stories/blogs/comedy would be boring.

3. Dig deeper into characters' motivations. Who are these people and why do they act the way they do?

4. Make more trips to the library. I only finish about one in three books I start, so I have to buy books regularly. I've been ordering from Powells and buying a mix of new and used. It's expensive, but I'm supporting other writers, so I don't feel bad about the money. Yet I need to supplement my purchases with more library books, titles that I'm uncertain about and new books I can't afford.

5. Read more literary fiction. Maybe read an occasional poem for inspiration. My writing is straightforward and lean and could benefit from an occasional poetic flair.

6. Conduct research interviews. Meet with law enforcement personnel and others in the community to develop background knowledge for future stories.

7. Listen carefully to beta readers. Be open to criticism and willing to fix problems. This is the point of having beta readers and why it's called a first draft.

8. Do not be in a hurry to submit. Let the manuscript sit untouched for a few weeks. Then revise the story with beta readers' comments in mind. Then send it out to other readers.

9. Start outlining my next novel. That way, I'll be writing it when the rejections start coming in. It's easier to think, *This next story will be the one*, if I'm in the process and feeling good about the new story.

10. Write new comedy material while I'm in between novels. It's hard work, but great fun at the same time. It's an important creative change of pace to get away from the serious crime stuff. Then go perform that material.

Elmore Leonard's Writing Rules

1. Never open a book with weather.
2. Avoid prologues.
3. Never use a verb other than *said* to carry dialogue.
4. Never use an adverb to modify the verb *said*.
5. Keep your exclamation points under control.
6. Never use the words *suddenly* or *all hell broke loose*.
7. Use regional dialect sparingly.
8. Avoid detailed descriptions of characters.
9. Don't go into great detail describing places and things.
10. Try to leave out the part that readers tend to skip.
11. If it sounds like writing, rewrite it.

Write What You Feel

Every time you read a novel, you get a peek into the writer's soul. Some authors are good at separating themselves from the story, especially if they write about a character completely unlike themselves. Jack Reacher, for example, who is not like Lee Child. Yet I believe that circumstances in each writer's life affect what they write, in a small way at least.

For example, if I have a headache when I'm writing, one of my characters will have a headache on the page that day, which I may later edit out. Or if I'm trying to lose weight, one of my minor characters will likely be in the same mode. Why not? Characters need realistic details to come to life on the page.

The pattern of transferring our own circumstances into the fiction we write happens on a much broader scale too. When I wrote *The Sex Club*, my son was in Iraq and I worried every day that he would die. My sister had just died of cancer and I grieved for her. So Kera, my main female protagonist, was dealing with those elements. Right or wrong, I couldn't separate those emotions from my writing and they ended up on the page.

Writing what you feel gives a story passion and realism that draws readers in. Yet there's a fine line that novelists have to be careful with. Earlier I mentioned Jack Reacher, a popular character for millions of crime fiction readers. He comes to mind because of a discussion on a listserv I participate in, which is what triggered this blog. Readers were discussing the author's last two stories. Some felt the character had changed too much, and others thought the writing had changed too much. It made me wonder if something significant had changed in the author's life. I have to mention here that most readers reported they loved both stories and that the author, Lee Child, is a very nice person who I've been fortunate to meet at Bouchercon.

But the listserv comments made me realize that readers notice changes in an author's style, and if they follow the author's personal life, they make connections. During the discussion, one list member said, "The writing reminds me of Robert Ludlum's novel just prior to his cardiac event. It didn't feel like a Ludlum novel..."

As an author, I hope to learn from this, but I'm realistic enough to accept that whatever is happening in my personal life will somehow affect what I write. Having just finished a fifth Jackson novel, I'm at a point of choosing what to write next. After five detective novels, I'm ready to try something new. Throw in five months of winter, and I'm feeling some cabin fever and crying out for a change of pace.

So I've decided to write a futuristic thriller, based on an outline I crafted a year ago. In reading back through the outline, I realize the theme of the novel is rather dark, and a year ago, I was at rock bottom in my novel-writing career. No coincidence.

Earlier this week, I took the first chapter to a critique group and they loved it, so I'm going to finish writing the story. Yet considering that my life and career are doing quite well now, I expect the ending to be more upbeat than I had originally planned.

Chapter 7: Promoting a Novel

Online Promotional Etiquette (8/08)

All this blogging and reading and commenting on other blogs has brought up a question about etiquette. Most comment sections identify the commenter by name only, whatever they've signed in as. My instinct is to include a link to one of my sites after my name or some kind of reference, such as: Author of *The Sex Club*. If someone likes what you said and wants to know more about you, your blog, or your books, it seems logical to let them know where to find you.

But I wonder: Is this socially acceptable in the blogosphere? A random survey of the blogs I visit indicates that most posters do not even include a full name signature, they just let the comment box identify them. Is it uncool to post a url? Does it depend on the blog site and how well you know the person?

Even though I've been participating in the online community for six months, I still feel like I don't know all the rules about promotion. Yesterday, for example, a woman on a mystery listserv said she was in a funk and couldn't get into any of the books she had at the house. So I sent her an email and offered to mail her a copy of

The Sex Club, then instantly wondered: *Was that improper?* Will that be considered blatant self-promotion and therefore, unwelcome? So I sent another email immediately afterward and apologized. She was not offended and sent back her mailing address. Yet it's so easy to cross this line. I know. I've done it...because I'm never sure where it is.

Especially after reading this post from another blog about online promotional etiquette: "You can't just barrel in and announce you're everyone's friend and aren't they lucky you have a book out now for everyone to buy. Well, you could. But I'm trying to be effective, not stupid. I get those emails a lot from people. I routinely delete them without reply. Every other blogger I talk to does the same thing. I see those kinds of posts on listservs I belong to, and I skim right over it as the ineffective mention that it is. The books I do mention on my blog, are by people I know, and like, and want to promote. The books I do notice on listservs are those talked about by actual readers as books they liked ..."

I'm the kind of person who usually doesn't hesitate to introduce myself or ask for something. I figure there's no harm in doing so. But now I wonder if I can do actual harm to my writing career if I cross the line too many times or offend the wrong person by sending an unwanted email. So what are the rules?

New Promotional Goals (8/08)

1. Give out more bookmarks! I read about people who say they do this everywhere and with everyone, and I must get into the habit. Goal: Give out three bookmarks a day. I intend to start ordering them in large quantities from online printers. Nothing like having 2,000 bookmarks sitting around to motivate you to give them away.

2. Send out one email a day to writer/mystery/review blogs offering to guest blog or participate in a Q&A.

3. Send out two emails a week to writers I know online (Facebook, CrimeSpace), offering a free copy of my novel. If they like it, they'll probably say so. Free promotion from other writers is as good as it gets.

4. Spend ten minutes a day on Goodreads in discussion forums and adding books to my list. This is a direct connection to readers.

5. Spend ten minutes a day on CrimeSpace. I used to do this every day, then got out of the habit when I started spending more time on Facebook and Twitter...and blogging every day. As a result, I've noticed a drop in the number of books I sell on Amazon.

6. Write one article a month and offer it to online magazines—even for no pay—just for exposure.

7. Use an Excel spreadsheet so I can track submissions and not get sloppy.

8. Get up earlier to get it all done!

Platform: Who Needs It? (6/09)

The buzzword for authors—or anyone marketing almost anything—is *platform*. Agents and editors all want their authors to have a platform, a tagline, something that sets them apart from everybody else.

First, what exactly does platform mean? According to the dictionary: "A body of principles on which a person or group takes a stand in appealing to the public" or "A place for public discussion; forum."

To marketers, more specifically, it means a specialty or subject in which you have expertise, a brand. For nonfiction writers, this concept is fairly straightforward. If I'm writing a book about training cats to line dance, then I must establish myself as an expert cat trainer— by blogging, giving talks to cat therapy groups, and writing articles for publications focused on all things feline.

But how does a fiction author establish a platform or brand? Cozy mystery writers give their characters specialties—knitting and rock collecting and what not.

Thus they have some basis for a platform and brand tagline: Dirk Daring, author of the Australian spelunking mysteries.

What if you write realistic crime stories? And each story is purposefully a little different, except for the featured regular-guy homicide detective? What sort of platform can you establish? Especially if you've never been a police officer, or pathologist, or crime scene tech in real life? What kind of tagline can you use that's distinct from hundreds of other crime writers? Can you really have a platform?

If you do find a way to make your stories or series unique and taggable, what happens when you start a new series or write a standalone or break out and write a futuristic thriller—all of which I hope to do someday. A new brand/tag for each endeavor? Or do you add to your original tagline as you go along?

The real question is: Do crime writers really need a platform? Or is being a little twisted enough of a specialty? How about a little truth in advertising?

- L.J. Sellers, author of the Detective Jackson mysteries, who also writes standalone suspense, futuristic thrillers, and the occasional husband-training manual.
- L.J. Sellers, closet deviant, masquerading as a novelist

Marketing Plans 101 (6/09)

A friend recently contacted me and asked for advice in developing a marketing plan—requested by a major book retailer as a condition of stocking her product. In today's publishing world, some smaller presses also expect authors to submit a marketing plan along with their novel. You should have one in place, anyway.

I'm certainly no expert, but I have developed several marketing plans, and I'm currently creating a new one for the September release of *Secrets to Die For*. In fact, I have two marketing plans: one to send to publishers and distributors, and one for myself to keep me on schedule.

My external marketing plan is organized by subject headers, such as the following. This example is just a framework and not a complete plan. I try to be as specific as possible, either providing a complete list or giving a specific number of contacts in my database.

Ongoing Online Efforts
- Blog twice a week
- Maintain/update author website
- Collect emails for newsletter
- Attend conferences such as Bouchercon
- Social networking through Facebook, Twitter, etc.

Send ARCS (include a complete list for each of these categories)
- Major reviewers (Publishers Weekly, Kirkus, etc.)

- Magazines (Ellery Queen, Crimespree, Entertainment Weekly, etc.)
- Newspapers (Washington Post, Register-Guard, etc.)
- Authors (list of authors you know who might read and blurb your book)
- Blogs (Reviewing the Evidence, Crime & Suspense)

Prepress Promotion
- Promotional flyers to mystery bookstores (90 in database), libraries (56 in database), and book clubs (75 in database)
- Promotional material to organizations/blogs with connections to book's content: For *The Sex Club*, I listed Planned Parenthood, NARAL, National Organization for Women
- Send out email announcement to list of 400 readers

Promotional Materials
- Print 500 bookmarks to give away at signings, conferences, etc.
- Print 100 promotional flyers giveaway at signings, conferences, etc.
- Other ideas: postcards, pens with book name, buttons

Advertising
- October: buy small ads with *Mystery Scene*, *Ellery Queen*, *Crimspree*
- Place online ad on The Graveyard Shift blog

Postpress Promotion

- Blog book tour (guest blog at 30 sites in 45 days)
- Guest blog regularly after book tour
- Book signings at 10 local bookstores (Borders, UO bookstore, Murder by the Book)
- Bookselling at several local book fairs (Art & the Vineyard, Lane County Fair)

Organizations

- Member of: Sisters in Crime, International Thriller Writers, Willamette Writers
- Send promotional material to each; get book into databases; participate in any promotional efforts available through membership

Timeline

- June: ARCs sent out
- July: promotional material prepared, printed
- August: promotional material and emails sent out
- September: blog tour and book signings
- October: blog tour, book signings, guest blogging

As I mentioned, I'm not an expert and have never taken any marketing seminars. I learned all this by reading, researching, watching other writers, and just doing it. My plans always include everything I'd like to do, but in reality I may not be able to afford it all.

My internal promotional plan for each release is organized by a timetable because that's the only way I can get it all done and stay on schedule. For a late

September release, it looks like the following. This also is just a framework and not a complete plan.

External Marketing Timeline (6/09)

June
1. Send ARCs to:
- Publishers Weekly, Kirkus, Booklist Mystery Magazine, New York Times Book Review, Washington Post, Entertainment Weekly, etc.
- Crime Spree, Ellery Queen, Mystery, other mystery magazines
- Mystery blogs (Reviewing the Evidence, Crime & Suspense, etc.)
- Select mystery bookstores
- Well-know authors (who I know)

2. Plan blog tour (make list of blogs to visit, map out subjects, contests, etc.)

July
- Send out emails for blog tour and set up schedule.
- Start writing blog tour posts (one a week, minimum)
- Print more bookmarks/send as giveaways to conferences everywhere
- Create and print promotional flyers for libraries, bookstores, and distributors
- Add to library database

- Update bookstore database
- Pass out bookmarks at Art & the Vineyard and Lane County Fair
- Design and print promotional flyers

August
- Send out promotional flyers to: 1) bookstores, 2) libraries, 3) book clubs
- Send press releases and advance review copies (ARCs) to local newspapers
- Set up book signings/book talks at bookstores in major towns in Oregon (Eugene, Portland, Salem, Medford, Ashland)
- Set up book talk at libraries
- Keep writing blog posts (one a week, minimum)
- Set up email/newsletter announcement with Vertical Response
- Get video trailer made (if money allows)

September
- Send publicity material to organizations: Willamette Writers, Backspace, International Thriller Writers, Sisters in Crime
- Send publicity information to related organizations
- Blog tour begins (drink lots of coffee and make no other plans)
- Send out email/newsletter to 400+ friends and readers the day the book is released

- Buy ads in mystery magazines and popular crime blogs

October
- Blog tour continues
- Book giveaway contests on blog and website
- Send out second round of promotional flyers or postcards (cheaper!) with new blurbs from reviewers
- Attend Bouchercon (hand out bookmarks, flyers, network)
- Post book trailer on as many sites as possible
- Attend Southern Oregon Book Festival

Author's current note: I have significantly revised my marketing plan in the last year to reflect a new focus on e-books.

Your Name Is Your Brand (5/10)

Marketers say consumers need to hear/see your name or product seven times before they decide to buy. Thus, we have branding. Getting your name out there over and over again. Authors should pay attention to this as well. If you use variations of your name on various websites just for fun, you're not making the most of branding.

True story about a friend of mine: I followed her on Twitter for months, where she used a different fun name, before I realized she was the same person I had met in another Yahoo group. Branding is most effective if you pick one name and stick with it everywhere. Less fun, admittedly, but we're not in this just for fun, are we?

Branding Basics (8/10)

Writers are all learning to be marketers. We promote and network and talk to readers, but branding is a little illusive. It goes hand in hand with platform, also a little squishy for a novelist to wrap her hands around. Still, the branding basics can be tweaked and modified and put to use for book promotion. Here are the fundamentals, which I copied from somewhere, and refer to on occasion.

1. Have enough passion about your brand/product that you appear alarming, maybe even almost creepy. (This one's easy for me.)

2. Know more about your topic/product/genre than 98% of the population. (I interview experts and do research for every novel. I also read everything I can about the publishing industry and crime fiction, in particular.)

3. Choose a brandable attribute somewhere between extraordinary and outright offensive. Stand out! (I've latched on to the words *provocative* and *mystery/suspense* to describe my stories. I could do more of this though.)

4. Treat your brand as if it were normal, not just a publicity stunt. (Yep. It's who I am. Everyday.)

5. Work yourself silly at branding for at least nine months, and up to three years. Don't quit during a lull. Only the tenacious survive. (I'm coming up on three years of 70-hour weeks and I see it paying off. Finally!)

6. Sell something while you're establishing your brand. Even if you think it's not working, stick with it and keep selling. (I've been selling all along and recently added three books to my portfolio.)

Writers as Salespeople (1/11)

A question from my ex-publisher inspired to me think about the pay structure in publishing. The question she asked was: *Why couldn't you sell all those books when you were still under contract?*

Many factors came into play at the same time that all pushed up my sales quickly. Pricing strategy, backlist books, and a massive effort to name a few. But one of the biggest issues was motivation, aka incentive.

In the business world, salespeople work for a small base pay and most of their income is in the form of incentive pay and bonuses. The more they sell, the more money they make. To some extent, this is true in traditional publishing, except that writers (aka salespeople) only get paid every six months. If other businesses functioned that way, they'd have a hard time hiring and keeping salespeople. It's really hard to stay motivated when you wait half a year for a paycheck...and then realize your publisher has kept most of it.

The other factor is information. Most salespeople get constant feedback on their performance. They know at any point exactly how their sales numbers are adding up. They can use that information to tailor their techniques and improve their sales. In traditional publishing, sales information comes too late to be effective and is often hard to decipher.

When you self-publish on Amazon, through both Kindle Direct and CreateSpace, after the initial six-week wait, you get paid every month. You also have access to hourly, daily, and monthly sales data. The information is direct feedback that can be used to figure out what promotional techniques work best.

Together, the steady income and the sales data, provide a great incentive to spend time every day blogging, tweeting, posting comments, and writing press releases. Wouldn't it be interesting if traditional publishing houses followed Amazon's lead and motivated their writers to be diligent salespeople as well?

Publishers will say: *It's not possible. It's too much bookkeeping. We've always done it this way*. But Amazon knows what it's doing, and it's kicking ass in the publishing world. Something to think about.

Book Promotion and Reader Trust (4/11)

Authors may feel pressured to invent new ways to promote their work, but unfortunately, some tactics are less ethical than others. We've all heard complaints from readers about five-star reviews written by the author's family, but now some novelists have taken Amazon-ranking manipulation to a new level by gifting books to readers.

What's wrong with giving away books? Nothing, in theory. I've given away hundreds of copies of my novels, both print and digital. But when an author gifts a book through Amazon, the transaction counts as a sale, and a lot of sales all at once can push a book higher in the rankings. Better visibility results in more sales. I understand the motivation to do this, yet it strikes me as deceptive. The practice leads readers to purchase the book based on the assumption that many other readers have already done so. If readers knew the author was the main buyer of those copies, they might make a different decision.

What is ethical and what is not? Having a friend or two read your book and post honest good reviews on various forums seems fine. For myself, I rarely solicit reviews, I've never asked anyone to post a review they didn't fully support, and none of my family members have ever posted reviews of my novels. At least not that I know about. If they're posting anonymously, it might explain a few things. ☺

But having friends post five-star reviews of a book they didn't read or didn't like is not okay. Directly giving away copies of your books in any format is great promotion and lots of fun, but buying your own books to manipulate the ranking is probably not a good idea.

As a guideline, I believe anything that would make a reader feel manipulated or lied to should be avoided. A lot of book promotion falls into a huge gray area of social networking and doesn't have clear boundaries. For example, it's typically okay to talk about your books if someone else brings them up, but readers hate it when writers sidetrack a discussion to talk about their own novels. They get annoyed when writers anonymously start discussions about their work. Writers can openly start discussions about their work...if they've been participating in the forum long enough to make friends. It's a delicate social balance.

Some readers have become super sensitive to this trend. Last month, a reader started a thread about my Jackson books, just because she loved the series and wanted to share her discovery. Another forum participant immediately assumed I, or someone connected to me, had initiated the thread. I've never done that and the complainer had no reason to believe I would, but clearly, enough authors engage in that sort of thing to make all of us look bad. I was delighted when other forum participants defended both me and my series, but the incident made me aware that writers as a group are developing a problem with reader trust.

Here's another gray area: When is it okay to add someone to your email database? I've always assumed if readers contact me about my novels or enter a contest to win a book, they'll expect me to add them to my newsletter file. Once they receive my mailing, which only goes out to announce new releases, they can immediately unsubscribe if they choose. Yet this is not a clear area, and some readers may not want to be emailed without explicit permission. I'm still grappling with the ethics of all this.

This subject could be endless, so I'll only bring up one more point. Writers who use Facebook and Twitter to exclusively promote their work do themselves more harm than good. It's spam. Sending people you don't really know invitations to read your work is also spam.

I'm not perfect, and I've made mistakes along the way. This post is intended to not only encourage authors to be ethical in their promotion but also to let readers know their trust is important to me.

Chapter 8: The Publishing Industry

Sex Sells . . . Or Does It? (4/08)

Sex sells. That's what marketers always say. And it seems to be true for tight-fitting jeans and toothpaste, but it is true in crime fiction? In my experience—not necessarily.

Some of the best reviews I received for my novel, *The Sex Club*, started out with a disclaimer like this: "I didn't think I would like this book, but . . ." The readers/reviewers went on to say the title (and sometimes the cover) had turned them away from the book and they'd read it reluctantly because another reader raved about it. They ended up loving the story, but still, their initial aversion concerned me.

After seeing the pattern, I asked members of Dorothly L (a reader/writer discussion forum) what they thought about the title. Many said they would never pick up the novel in a bookstore or library because of the title. So then I wondered: How many bookstores and libraries had decided not to stock the novel because of the title? From the comments of a few, I believe there might be many. After realizing this painful reality, I started adding this footnote to all my communications about the novel: *Despite the title, the story isn't X-rated.*

It is not a good sign when you have to explain or make excuses for your title.

On the other hand, many writers on the CrimeSpace and Facebook networking sites have posted great comments about *The Sex Club's* cover and title. One writer posted, "Judging by the title, that's a book I HAVE to read RIGHT NOW." Many others have simply said, "Love the cover!" and "I love the title!" Some even commented that they liked the book's short pitch on Amazon: *A dead girl, a ticking bomb, a Bible study that's not what it appears to be, and a detective who won't give up.*

But when I started a discussion specifically asking how they felt about the word *sex* in a crime fiction title, the reaction was mixed. One writer said, "If sex is in the title, isn't that a lot of emphasis, leading the buyer to think the book might be in the wrong section of the bookstore?" Another commented, "For me, the word *sex* would have to be relevant to the plot. I hate titles that just try to get people to buy even when it has nothing whatsoever to do with the story."

Yet another writer posted, "Several years ago a thriller came out called *The Sexual Occupation* of Japan by Richard Setlowe. It got a starred review in PW but didn't do too well sales-wise."

In a similar online discussion, many people (mostly women) said they simply skip sex scenes when they come across them in mystery/suspense stories. I also feel they drag down a fast-paced story, which is why I didn't write any such scenes in the novel.

My publicist, who came on board after the book had been printed, felt very strongly that the title was a mistake and made both of our jobs a lot harder than they needed to be. She thought that not only was I turning off mystery readers but also alienating other readers who were attracted to the title, then disappointed to find out the book didn't have much sex in it.

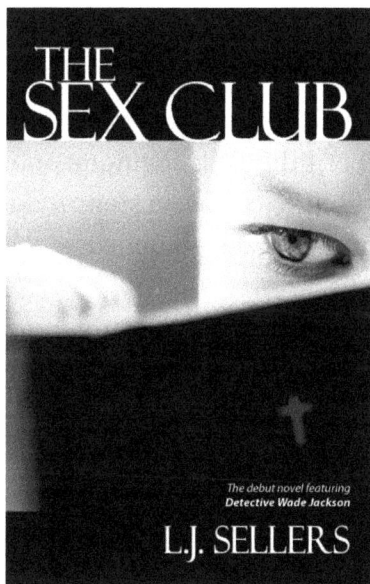

I've come to believe she's right. A quick search of Amazon brought up only one other mystery title with the word *sex* —*Sex and Murder* (A Paul Turner Mystery). But at least that author was smart enough to get the word *murder* in the title too. Mystery readers love a good murder! I'm sure there may be others, but after months of perusing thousands of reader postings on multiple listservs, I've yet to see another mystery title mention sex.

I debated the name, *The Sex Club*, for months, and finally went with it because it seemed perfect for the story. And to be honest, I thought it might get media attention. But in retrospect, if I had it to do all over again, I'd change it. My conclusions: 1) Bookstores and libraries are critical to sales, and authors can't afford to alienate them or their patrons, 2) Mystery readers prefer dead bodies to warm ones.

Fixing the Publishing Industry Is No Mystery (1/09)

Jean asked if I was worried about the downturn in the publishing industry and what I think can be done about it. The fix isn't a mystery at all. Three basic steps would change the industry's business model to improve sales and cut costs.

1. Move away from the hardback fiction book. Publishers could simply not print hardbacks and let libraries and collectors laminate their own copies of trade paperbacks, or they could print very limited hardback runs with the bulk of the first printing done in trade or mass market paperback. Then the first run of each novel could be bigger and priced to reach the whole market. Publishers win by reducing their printing costs and minimizing the number of returns. Readers win by getting a book they can afford when it first comes out, and writers win by reaching as wide a market as they can on the first publication. And if publishers produced an e-book version at the same time, it would open the market even further. Writers who didn't hit the big numbers would never be stuck with a book that was only available in hardback—a spendy version that's hard to sell at book fairs and special events, which limits sales even further.

2. Change distribution to a nonreturnable basis. This seems like such a no brainer. Approximately 25%–40% of all books printed are returned and shredded. This is an unsustainable waste of time and resources. Once the new policy was in place, bookstores would have to be conservative about how many books they ordered at one time, but it would simplify the bookkeeping for everyone involved—especially authors who often have their royalties held back against returns.

3. Print only as many copies as necessary to fill orders. Yes, there is a discount in volume, but if, in the long run, the model isn't making money, it only makes sense to pay a slightly higher per-unit printing cost and have fewer returns. Money (and trees) would be saved from not printing, shipping, processing, and shredding books that never sell.

If all that happened, bookstores would have fewer returns to process and they could make money by remaindering books in the store. They could offer discounts and "buy one/get one free" deals to keep product moving. Publishers could cut their printing (and shredding) costs and spend more money on promotion for more authors, not just the bestsellers.

This would take the pressure off each novel to perform to a certain standard and allow more novels to come to the market through traditional publishers.

Of course, this advice is aimed at the major publishers, which still control the bulk of the market. Many smaller publishers have already employed some of these ideas. But they can't work on a large scale unless they're widely adopted. As long as the hardback book carries a certain prestige, publishers (and authors) who only have paper versions will remain at a disadvantage.

Digital ARCs Are Making Progress (12/09)

Simon & Schuster is the newest publisher to offer digital ARCs (advanced review copies) directly to reviewers, media, bloggers, journalists, librarians, and booksellers. So far, the galleys are available by email invitation only, but early readers can register for consideration. I expect more publishers will follow. Others, such as Clarkson Potter, a Random House imprint, have already been experimenting with e-galleys.

NetGalley, which started early this year, is a central website where publishers can invite contacts to view their print or digital galleys, and readers can request galleys they want to review. The service is free to the early readers I just mentioned, plus educators. I haven't heard much about this site, so I'm interested in feedback from people or publishers who have used it.

Nxtbook, another new company, is a web-based provider of digital content such as e-galleys and e-magazines as an alternative option for subscribers. I love it that we're moving away from paper for disposable reading experiences.

It may take a while for the major reviewers— *Publishers Weekly, Library Journal, Kirkus, The New York Times*—to start accepting e-galleys, but it seems inevitable that they will. The pressure will come from within, all those employers/reviewers who are hooked on their Kindles and other e-readers will start to resent lugging around those paper galleys.

Not every early reader in the industry has an e-reader, but many do. The savings on printing and postage will be huge. The cost and time savings will benefit small, overworked publishers the most. The convenience for early readers will translate to more books being read and reviewed before publication. I believe this is good for writers.

Random Thoughts About the Industry (5/10)

One-star protest. The Kindle reader practice of giving a book a one-star Amazon review to protest the price or publisher's business contract has to go. It's like stiffing a waiter or complaining about the service because you're pissed off about the price of your meal or the restaurant's policies. It punishes the wrong people and in the long run, is probably a waste of time. Amazon set up the star rating system, and it can take it down if the system is abused. If you don't like the price, don't buy the book. Stop hurling tomatoes at the author.

Do-it-yourself publishing. It seems the self-publishing trend on Kindle and Smashwords will eventually hurt the vanity presses. A certain number of writers may always be willing to pay someone else to turn their Word document into a book —and keep a good chunk of the profit—but that number must be dwindling. Writers can find someone to format their books for Kindle and Smashwords fairly cheaply. Those who want a printed book can go through CreateSpace for next to nothing. How will vanity presses survive in this new world of do-it-yourself publishing? For that matter, now long will the major publishers survive? I think independent presses will be the last ones standing.

Agents and Bookstores as Publishers? (5/10)

There's been a lot of game-changing industry news lately, but some interesting developments that caught my eye were buried in a report under Joe Konrath's deal with Amazon Encore. In a nutshell: agents and bookstore are becoming publishers.

Scott Waxman, of Waxman Literary, has created Diversion Books, a separate business from his literary agency that is similar to Amazon Encore and is "somewhere in between the big houses and the lonely road of self-publishing." The company, which currently has about 20 projects signed up, offers e-book publication and distribution as well as POD, with a focus on the e-book frontlist.

Waxman says Diversion Books will take on authors who cannot sell books in numbers that make financial sense for the major houses. "If you have an author with a platform who can sell books, we're happy selling 5,000 to 10,000 copies," he said in the report.

Bookstores are getting into the act too. Susan Novotny, owner of the Book House of Stuyvesant Plaza, Albany, N.Y., will launch Staff Picks Press, a new indie publishing house. "Independent booksellers have been making readers aware of good novels for a long time," says Novotny in an interview. "We have over 40 reading groups connected to our stores… and my staff… recommends the books they love all day long. Now, some of those books will come directly from us."

Agents are also advising their clients in new ways: As reported: Ted Weinstein, of Ted Weinstein Literary Management, said he's now having a conversation with all of his clients about the smartest way to publish their books—and going with a big house isn't a foregone conclusion. "Authors can now be more self-possessed," he said. "They can go with a major house, an agency, or one of the turnkey services from a major retailer, whether it's Lulu, Blurb, Amazon, or now B&N."

Speaking of Barnes & Noble. Now that it's in direct competition with Amazon for self-published digital books, why not take the next step and start publishing its own titles too? Amazon is already doing it and so are other bookstores, such as Book House mentioned early and Poison Pen Press, the front runner for this idea.

Big publishers are 1) buying/releasing fewer books, 2) expecting agents and authors to do more editing, 3) using outside public relations firms, 4) making authors primarily responsible for their own marketing, 5) offering smaller advances, 6) cancelling popular series that don't meet a quota, and 7) pissing off digital readers by holding back e-books and overpricing them.

What's left to like? Oh yes, they still have the advantage for distribution. But when Borders folds and B&N starts filling its shelves with toys and games, as it already plans to do, big publishers will have less of an edge in distribution.

It seems inevitable authors will begin to gravitate to small and midsize publishers, including those run by their favorite bookstores and agents—publishers that release trade paper books in small POD runs and in e-book formats at the same time. These authors will forgo advances in exchange for more control of their work and greater royalties on each book.

This is a terrific time to be an author. The brass ring may be harder to attain, but there are more choices than ever and a lot of happy places in the middle.

Still Holding Out (2/11)

I hear from authors every day—Facebook friends, writers who read my blogs or novels, people I meet at conferences. They often ask about my indie e-book publishing experience, then many close the exchange by saying, "But I'm still holding out for a traditional publisher." I politely make no comment.

On one level, I understand this. A publishing contract is a writer's dream and it's hard to let go of. But as the industry goes through a major upheaval, writers need to ask themselves: What is more important? Having a traditional publisher or making money? Being one of the chosen or having thousands of people read my book? Some authors seem to have it all, but most midlist writers are already facing these choices.

Just how long should you hold out for a publisher?

After twenty years of having major publishers (and film producers) say, "I love this story, but I'm not going to buy it," I finally self-published my first novel, a police procedural called *The Sex Club*. I released it in a traditional way and many people, including reviewers, never knew it was self-published. After the book gained traction, I found a small press to pick up the series. That was late 2008, and I still thought I needed a publisher for respectability. I soon came to realize that having a small publisher was more of a liability than an asset.

Here's why:

1. There is nothing a small publisher can or will do for writers that they can't do better for themselves. I don't mean literally do each thing yourself, but authors can contract for production services as well as a publisher can. Small presses are often run by a few dedicated, but overworked individuals, who typically contract out most services and pay bottom dollar. As an author, you can shop around and find the best editor/graphic designer/e-book formatter you can afford.

2. A small publisher will not have a sales staff or a distribution network (no bookstores) and is not likely to spend any money promoting your book. What a small publisher will do is potentially overprice your book and keep most of the profit of the few hundred books you manage to sell on your own.

There may still be some advantages to signing with a large press. An advance can buy time to write another book, and the Big 6 publishers can get your novel into bookstores. But as the author, you have to sell the book no matter who publishes it. Meanwhile, chain bookstores are closing and Borders is going bankrupt, so the distribution network is crumbling. That advantage won't mean much in a few years, especially since e-books are capturing more and more of the market.

What's left for the author is the label of being *traditionally published* and the convenience of having someone else contract the production work. Giving up most of the profit for those small advantages is a crappy bargain I finally decided I was done with.

Early last year after being laid off from my job, I realized something had to change and I took a hard look at my own situation. No matter which way I looked at it, I kept coming back to the idea that self-publishing e-books was the only way to save my career and my house.

So I left my publisher and released all of my completed stories as e-books. In January, I had one book on Kindle and sold 31 copies. In December, I had six books on Kindle and sold more than 10,000. I also worked like a maniac at production and promotion for eight months to make it happen. I had set a goal of making a living from e-books by mid 2011, and I got there considerably faster than I dreamed.

So far, the numbers and the reviews keep getting better. In April, I'll release my fifth Detective Jackson novel, and for the first time, thousands of readers are eagerly waiting for it. For me, that is significantly more rewarding than industry approval.

I've Seen the Future, and It's Not That Scary
(6/11)

The changes in publishing are happening so fast and furious, it's almost surreal. If someone had predicted this stuff even five years ago, people would have scoffed and called it social-science fiction. Here's a recap of the last two weeks:

- Amazon launched a fifth publishing imprint, Thomas & Mercer, which will focus on mysteries and thrillers. Its first four titles will be available on the Kindle, in print and audio formats at amazon.com, as well as in bookstores.
- Amazon hired former Time Warner Books CEO and current agent Larry Kirshbaum to head Amazon Publishing's New York office, putting Amazon in direct competition with NY publishers.
- Amazon has asked publishers to start submitting books in epub format, paving the way for standardization of digital books. Readers and authors rejoice!
- Liberty Media, a cable conglomerate, offered to buy Barnes & Noble, and most analysts say it's on the strength of the retailer's e-reader (Nook) and plans to expand into global digital markets.

You'll note that three of those announcements involve Amazon, and all involve e-books. As someone who's currently writing a futuristic thriller, I've been thinking a lot about the future 13 years from now. In addition to the dystopian elements I've included in my novel, I try to imagine realistic changes in business and commerce. The one thing that seems inevitable is that Amazon will become a huge, media-and-retail conglomerate that wields megapower. In my current reality, I survive on the royalties I receive from Amazon for my e-books sales.

What does all this mean? For starters, if you can, buy stock in Amazon. ☺ And if you still want to sign a contract with a publisher, Amazon should be your first choice. I also think traditional publishing will consolidate to the point that there may only be two or three main presses, and I expect Amazon and B&N to be the dominant forces because they control distribution. B&N is likely to follow Amazon's lead (as it has done with Nook and PubIt!) and enter the traditional publishing business, signing with authors to release books in all formats and also with e-book exclusivity clauses. This could be a negative for readers because some titles will be available only on Kindle, and some titles will be available only on Nook.

The good news for readers is that there will eventually be more standardization of e-book formats. A few years from now, any e-book you buy will be readable on every device you own... unless it was published by the competition.

For writers, it means you will either get picked up by one of the Big 3, with a much better deal than any Big 6 press ever offered, or you'll go it alone and promote like hell. Small presses will likely disappear too.

I also believe e-book prices are going to drop significantly in the near future, driven by Amazon's dominance as a volume retailer and by self-published authors' drive to gain readership. As a reader, this is good news. As a writer, it's the one thing that makes me the most nervous.

Does Reader Engagement Go Too Far?

Being a middle child, and a nice person, and a workaholic, I've spent my life trying to do the right thing and make people happy. As a member of a dysfunctional family, I've given up the goal, but as a novelist, I'm still trying to satisfy my current readers while reaching out to new ones. Some days though, I'm not sure what I should be doing.

The new catch phrases in marketing are *content* and *engagement*. Content seems easy: just keep writing stories that people want to read. But the experts say that's not enough. They say I need to pen informative blogs, write short stories to give away, and create entertaining videos. So I'm doing all that.

Engaging readers is a less-concrete concept and I'm starting to think the idea is more hype than practicality. For example, a well-read post recently advised authors to do the following:

Listen—Create ways to listen to your readers and collect data about what you hear; use focus groups and surveys to support regular listening mechanisms.

Customer knowledge—Find out why people buy your products (or not), why they recommend you to others (or not), and why they are repeat buyers. Understand what else they buy. Understand who your buyers are, what segment and communities they belong to.

Conversations—Find unique ways of connecting with readers, ways that will enhance your brand as an author, ways that enable dialogue, not one-way broadcast.

Collaborate—Go beyond listening and conversation to collaborate with your readers, perhaps testing your products in advance of a full launch or soliciting ideas for additional content.

Long-term relationships—Develop mechanisms to foster long-term connections with your readers. Keep them engaged even as you create new offerings.

Community—Build a community of your readers. Facilitate mechanisms for readers to interact with one another as part of this community and to broaden the reach to additional readers.

Some of this is intuitive and I'm already doing it. But surveys? As a consumer, I hate surveys, and I'm not likely to ever clutter my readers' in-boxes with a questionnaire. Collaborate? Meaning, ask readers where they'd like me to take the series or characters? I'd get as many different answers as there are readers.

In fact, that's the biggest problem with engagement. Some readers like to interact with authors. They send emails, go to conferences, and participate in online discussions. Many readers, perhaps the majority, would rather not engage with the author. They simply want to read the books and move on. I've heard some readers say they don't even like seeing an author bio in a novel, because they enjoy the story more if they don't know anything about the author.

I understand and respect this. I also love readers who contact me to talk about my stories. So I'm trying to find the middle ground and make all my readers happy...without wasting time on activities that readers will ignore or find annoying.

Are Pen Names Pointless? (8/11)

The publishing industry is in upheaval with major changes, but one of the more subtle changes is the declining use of pen names. As more authors take charge of their own publishing and online marketing, they choose to skip the pen names when they write in various genres, in an effort to capitalize on the brand success of the name they're already selling under.

This makes sense to me, and it's why I'm publishing my futuristic thriller, *The Arranger*, under the same author name as my police procedurals. Essentially, the books are all crime stories, and in this case, they even share a major character, so I never considered using a pen name. Some marketers would argue this is a mistake, but I disagree.

In fact, even if I decided to write in a completely different genre, say fantasy, I still don't think I would use a pen name. Here's why. Marketers at major publishing houses established the practice with the idea that books should be categorized and shelved by genre and that readers were easily confused. They worried readers would buy a book in a genre they didn't want just because it had their favorite author's name on it.

This seems like an insult to readers. If the cover art and book description are doing their jobs, then readers will know exactly what the genre is and what to expect from the novel—regardless of the name on the cover. Readers have also come to expect authors to pen stories in various genres. It is neither surprising, nor confusing to them.

In addition, writers are blending story types and making up their own genres. Paranormal historical mystery, anyone? Or in my case: futuristic crime thriller. I'm not sure pen names were ever useful, but if they were, readers are long past it. In the age of the internet and open access to writers, readers learn everything they need to about an author and their various books with a quick visit to their website.

What about readers browsing in bookstores? Does a pen name prevent them from buying a futuristic police procedural written by J.D. Robb instead of a romance by Nora Roberts? I don't think so. At least not more than once. I know there are instances in which a pen name could be useful, such as if the author wants or needs privacy, but those cases are rare.

To minimize any possible confusion, I labeled my novel with a subtitle: A Futuristic Thriller, and I created a different style of cover. It will be clear to my Detective Jackson fans that this novel is different from my police procedurals.

I also have two other standalone thrillers, so most of my readers already know that I write non-Jackson books. Of course, I want my Jackson fans to try the new novel, which is partially why I sent Detective Lara Evans into the future to tell this story. (I also think she's a lot of fun, but that's another blog.)

Some of my police procedural readers will check out this novel and some will pass. That's okay. I'm hoping new readers who've never heard of me will try it too.

As a fairly new author, I have to capitalize on my name recognition. My name is my brand. Without the support of a major publisher, it's all I have, and I use it everywhere: Facebook, Twitter, chat groups, etc. I never use amusing nicknames like *thrillergirl* or *crimefighter*. They might be fun, but they don't tell readers who I am. I'm not likely to ever use a pen name either, for the same reasons.

Chapter 9: The E-Book Revolution

The Rise of E-Books (2/09)

As the Kindle 2 is unveiled, the buzzword in publishing is e-book, e-book, e-book. It's the only segment of the industry in which sales are growing, and this phenomenon has some readers worried—"I'll miss the feel and smell of a new book"—while others are delighted—"The environmental benefits are worth the sacrifice."

But what does it mean to authors? Speculation on that front is rampant as well. 1) "More new authors will be published because the production costs are so minimal." 2) "Author advances will disappear, and it will be more difficult to earn a living as a novelist." 3) "If you don't have an e-book, you're missing a whole section of the market. All three scenarios could come true."

Another interesting question: Will e-books fall into the same categories—traditionally published versus self-published—that print books do? Will novels from well established e-publishers automatically carry more prestige than an e-book from Author Unknown? I read a post today that stated unequivocally that one of the benefits of publishing an e-book is: "You don't have to go through the obstacles and headaches involved in finding an agent and a publisher."

What about distribution? If you don't go though the headache of finding an e-book publisher, how will anyone find and buy your book? Just because your book is downloadable from your website or for sale on Amazon doesn't guarantee that you'll have buyers. The production quality and file choice matter too. You want your e-book to be downloadable to the major e-readers: Kindle, Sony, and Mobipocket Reader.

I've thought about all of this because I've considered self-publishing some of my early novels as e-books. Then I decided against it because the benefit would be minimal and the stigma of being a self-published e-book author would be great. I know that statement will rile some people, but the stigma is real, whether deserved or not. Well-known authors, on the other hand, could probably do quite well selling e-books from their own websites.

Ultimately, as an author, I want to have all my books available both in print and e-files from traditional publishers with established distribution (and web traffic). But the publishing industry is changing and becoming less clearly defined. As e-book sales grow and become a sizable chunk of the market, some of the old distinctions may disappear.

Taking the Plunge

I finally took the plunge! Many traditionally published authors have self-published their backlist titles and/or unsold manuscripts as e-books, and now I've joined them in this exciting venture. Why not?

Before I started writing the Detective Jackson series, I wrote several standalone thrillers, both with a subtle medical theme. (I was a senior editor on a pharmaceutical magazine for years and medical information fascinates me!) I had a terrific agent for the stories, so I know they're marketable, and it's exciting to finally get them out there for readers to enjoy.

The first, *The Suicide Effect*, is on Kindle now, but will also be available as a print book, mostly through Amazon. Here's the back cover copy:

When Sula overhears a shocking revelation about a drug being developed by her employer, she's paralyzed with indecision. She desperately needs her job to gain the judge's favor in a custody hearing for her son, yet hundreds of patient lives could be at stake. Two days later when the drug's lead scientist disappears, Sula is compelled to search for the incriminating data. But Prolabs' CEO is a desperate man determined to stop her. Can Sula get the proof and expose the drug's fatal flaw before the CEO risks everything to silence her?

My early readers say it's a unique and compelling story with terrific characters. I hope you'll check it out. Very shortly, I'll release a second thriller, *The Baby Thief*, a novel unlike any you've ever read. I'll have more details when the book is ready. What you do think? Am I crazy to do this?

5 Ways to Read an E-Book (9/10)

Several readers have emailed me and said, *I'd really like to read your e-books, but I don't know how…* Which inspired me to put together this list.

1. Buy an e-reader: Kindle is the most popular, but there's also the Nook, Kobo, Sony Pocket Reader, Pandigital Novel, and many more. When you make your choice, think about more than device and price. Think about the size of the bookstore available to you and the size/power/longevity of the company behind the bookstore and device (e.g., Amazon). Prices are way down, so why wait?

2. Download the Kindle to your Mac or PC. With this application you can shop the Kindle store and read Kindle books on your computer or laptop or iPad. (As info: Kindle books are mobi files.)

3. Do you use Firefox? It has a built-in e-reader. Click on the Tools menu and open the ePub-Catalog. You can drag epub files from your computer into the e-reader and peruse them there. (As info: Almost everybody but Amazon uses epub files.)

4. Read on your iPad. You can shop the Apple store directly and buy e-books from it, or download the Kindle application to your iPad. Some readers love reading on the iPad, and others say it gives them a headache.

5. If you buy or win a PDF file from an author, you can read it on your computer, laptop, or mobile phone—or send it to your e-reader.

Free E-Books or Not? (9/10)

I've been debating whether to offer one of my books for free on Kindle, temporarily, as a promotion. I know other authors have used the tactic successfully, and I have given away hundreds of print books and done so happily. But I keep talking myself out of doing a free Kindle e-book. Why?

The free downloads on Kindle have picked up a negative association, and if I don't value my books, how can I expect readers to?

Here's a reader comment from the Amazon Kindle forum: *Since I realized most of the free books are junk, I've removed them from my kindle. I wouldn't have written this except it bugs me that these books are showing up on the bestseller lists for Kindle. So I guess the best way is to do all my searches under the DTB [dead tree book] bestseller listings and then, if I find something there that looks good, hope that it is on Kindle also.*

I've seen lots of posts that refer to free books as junk and other negative terms. Even the readers who do download them, don't value them. They often stick them in a Someday folder, to be read after everything else. Readers place more value on the books they purchase.

Here's another forum comment: *I generally just take a quick look at the "free list" because sometimes a real book is free for a day or two as a teaser from the publisher; otherwise I don't bother.*

Note the expression *real book*. This reader doesn't consider free indie books to be real books by real authors.

Rather than risk being lumped into that category, I've decided to keep selling my e-books at the very reasonable price of $2.99. I may not be premium, but I'm worth something.

E-Book Self-Publishing Roundup
(Written 1/11, updated 7/11 for *The Writer* magazine)

Amazon: Kindle Direct Publishing

Amazon pioneered the e-book publishing revolution and commands a reported 75% of e-book sales, so its Kindle Direct Publishing (KDP) platform is the place to start. The online retailer uploads its KDP content directly to the Kindle bookstore. After opening an account, authors can upload a Word, HTML, or PDF file, which Amazon converts to a mobi file that can be read by the Kindle device. Don't be intimidated by the term, it's just a type of software. Authors can also create their own mobi file or hire a professional to create it, a step that ensures a quality, easy-to-read product.

If you want your cover to be part of your e-book, it must be integrated with your text, regardless of which software you use. The KDP site allows you to upload the cover file separately with your product description, but that image displays on Amazon's bookstore, not in your actual e-book.

For books priced between $2.99 and $9.99, Amazon pays a 70% royalty. For everything else, it pays 35% of the list price. Authors can price their books as they choose (with a 99-cent minimum), but Amazon reserves the right to discount. To keep the 70% royalty, authors can't sell their e-book for less anywhere else. If you do, Amazon's web crawlers will quickly discover the lower price and discount your book on the Amazon site. If the price falls below $2.99, the Amazon royalty drops from 70% to 35%, so be careful how you price your book for other distributors.

Originally, most Kindle titles were purchased by people who owned the Kindle e-reader, but Amazon has now released applications that let anyone who owns a computer, mobile phone, or iPad download Kindle books to read on their device of choice. The only places readers can't buy Kindle books are from Amazon's retail competitors, such as Borders and Barnes & Noble. Authors can chose to publish with or without digital content management (DRM), which protects files from piracy but is also unpopular with some readers.

After an initial waiting period of six weeks, Amazon pays monthly and deposits royalties directly into the author's bank account. Authors can track their real-time sales, including UK and Germany sales, through their KDP bookshelf. No start-up fee is required.

Smashwords

Founded by entrepreneur Mark Coker, the website was originally designed to sell authors' digital content directly to online customers, but Smashwords now also distributes to many e-readers, including Kindle, Sony, Nook, and Kobo, and to other devices such as iPad and iPhone.

The site requires authors to upload their books as Word documents that have been properly formatted according to Smashword's guidelines. Authors often complain about the difficulty of getting the formatting correct. In addition, readers often complain about the "ugliness" of e-books produced by Smashwords' software. For authors who want complete control of the way their e-book is formatted and presented, Smashwords may not be the best choice.

On the other hand, it has no set-up fee, and authors can price their book (or other content) as they like, including offering it for free and providing discount coupons for special promotions. For content directly from its site, Smashwords pays an 85% royalty, minus discounts and processing fees. It offers a 70.5% royalty for sales through its affiliates. All content is published without DRM.

Smashwords pays authors on a quarterly basis, within 40 days after the close of each quarter. You can choose to receive either a paper check or a payment through PayPal, but authors must accrue $75 in royalties before a check will be issued and a minimum of $10 in royalties for an e-payment. Authors can track their real-time sales on the site's dashboard. Most authors report that their Smashword sales are only 10% or less of their Kindle sales, but the site is a one-stop distribution platform that reaches many retail markets.

Barnes & Noble's PubIt!

The retail bookseller launched this platform in mid-2010 and publishes an author's work directly to Barnes & Noble's e-bookstore, which also supplies the Nook e-reader. Following Amazon's model, B&N pays a 65% royalty on books priced between $2.99 and $9.99 and pays 40% on everything else. Authors can set their own list price, but B&N reserves the right to offer a retail discount to customers.

The PubIt! site takes uploads of epub files only, but it also offers a tool that coverts Word, HTML, RTF and TXT files, and it provides formatting guides that will help you create an attractive epub file. As yet, there is no standardization in e-books. Most e-readers handle epub files, but Amazon's Kindle only reads mobi files, so self-published authors will likely need to produce both types. But recent Amazon announcements indicate that may soon change.

As with Kindle Direct, authors can choose to employ digital rights management or not, but with B&N, once an author has made the choice, he or she can't reverse the decision for that file. To make changes to the content, authors must correct the epub file and upload it again. Cover art can be included in the epub file and also uploaded separately to display on the website's product description.

B&N pays monthly to the author's bank account 60 days after the end of the sales month and does not charge a set-up fee. The only platform to do so, PubIt! requires authors to supply a credit card number when setting up their account. Most venues also require authors to provide a social security number so they can report earnings to the IRS.

BookBrewer

Its partnership with the now-defunct Borders may be over, but BookBrewer assures writers that it's still going strong and its content continues to be available. This venue may be the easiest to use for authors who have few technical skills, because it lets them copy and paste almost any text content, including blogs (RSS feeds), into its software to create epub files.

Like Smashwords, BookBrewer distributes its content to various devices, such as e-readers, the iPhone, the iPad, and Android-powered tablets, but there is a price to pay for that full distribution. The company offers three publishing packages. For $19.99, it creates an e-book (with ISBN) from your document and distributes it to online retailers. For $29.99, it creates an e-book (without ISBN) and gives it to you to upload or sell anywhere. For $39.99, it combines those services and 1) creates an e-book (with ISBN), 2) gives you a copy to sell or give away as you like, and 3) distributes your book to other retailers.

BookBrewer pays 95% of post-retail royalty. Meaning, retailers take their percentages and fees—which can be as high as 65%—off the top of the book price, and BookBrewer pays the author 95% of what it earns. It pays through PayPal on a quarterly basis, 45 days after it receives payment from retailers and after the author earns at least $25 in royalties.

INscribe Digital (http://www.ingrooves.com/inscribe)

A subsidiary of INgrooves, INscribe Digital is a distribution company for authors who have five or more titles. Authors must supply both mobi and epub files to INscribe, which distributes the books to various retailers and e-readers, including Kindle, Kobo, Nook, and Sony. It also distributes to iPads, iPhones, and various other devices. The company is currently setting up distribution to libraries as well and is always on the lookout for new retail venues. For authors who want a one-stop experience, this could be a good choice.

Authors set their own prices and choose where they want to sell their books. For example, authors can opt out of distribution to Amazon if they already have a Kindle Direct account. As a distributer with hundreds of books, INscribe can negotiate higher royalties than an individual author may be offered. The company charges a $50 set-up fee per book and keeps 5% of all royalties. It pays authors once a month, but an author must earn at least $200 before a royalty check will be issued.

As e-book sales continue to escalate, more self-publishing platforms will enter the market. For example, authors can now distribute their books through BookBee based in Australia (bookbee.net). Savvy self-published authors will stay on the lookout for new opportunities to reach readers wherever they are or however they read their digital files.

Investing in Your Own E-Book (1/11)

After publishing six e-books in 2010, I've come to two conclusions:

1. Digital self-publishing is a straightforward process that isn't particularly difficult or expensive.

2. There is nothing a small publisher can or will do for writers that they can't do better for themselves. I don't mean literally do everything yourself, but a writer can contract for production services as well as a publisher can.

Why? Small presses are often run by a few dedicated, but overworked individuals. They typically contract out most services, and they often pay bottom dollar. I know this because I've worked as a freelance editor and turned down all of the work offered by small presses because they simply don't pay enough. Small presses are trying to profit and survive like everyone else and they cut costs where they can.

A large publisher can offer distribution and promotional backing, but most small publishers don't offer either, so what's left for the author is the label of being *traditionally published* and the convenience of having someone else contract the production work. Giving up most of the profit for these small advantages is a hard bargain that I don't recommend. As the author, you have to sell the book no matter who publishes it, so you might as well make the investment, publish it yourself, and reap the rewards

The three main elements to producing a quality e-book are editing, cover design, and formatting. Many authors are tempted to do all three themselves to save money. But unless you're incredibility talented and have all the time in the world, it's probably not a cost-effective decision.

Editing can be expensive, especially if you contract for content evaluation, but you can keep the cost down by sending your manuscript to beta readers or working with a critique group to fine tune the plot and structure. You should, of course, print and read the manuscript out loud before paying anyone else to proof it. After carefully reading it yourself, send it to a professional editor for line editing and proofreading. Many editors charge $1500 and up, but you don't have to pay that much. You can find someone to proofread your manuscript for $300–$800, depending on the length of the novel. If you pay less, your editor will be in a rush and probably won't do a good job. If you pay more, it may take a long time to earn back your investment.

A good cover is also essential. Most cover artists charge a flat fee, and you can expect to pay between $150 and $500. Some charge a lot more than that, but why spend that much if you don't have to? One way to save money is to find the right image yourself, so you're not paying the artist for that time. One of the great things about self-publishing an e-book is that you can revise it as often as you want, including creating a new cover down the road when the book is making money. The best way to find a cover designer is to network with other writers, including joining listservs that focus on marketing.

Formatting: I originally thought I would learn to format my own e-books to save money. Other authors make it sound easy. But I quickly decided the time and frustration spent on the learning curve was not cost-effective. Time is money. For me, it made more sense to send my Word files and cover jpgs to a professional for formatting. The e-book I got back was gorgeous. In fact, I received two files: a mobi file to upload to Amazon and an epub to upload everywhere else. I strongly recommend working with a formatter who produces these two types of files.

Readers' biggest complaint about e-books is the formatting. Getting it right is essential. Rates may vary, but if you're starting with a Word document, it shouldn't cost more than around $150. For authors who have a backlist and novels that are in book form instead of Word documents, those books will need to be scanned, and the cost of e-book production will be more expensive. The number of errors from the optical character recognition is also much higher. It might be cost-effective to pay a very fast typist to transcribe your published book into a Word document before sending it to a formatter. You'll end up with fewer errors too.

Taking the lowest rates I've mentioned ($300, $150, and $150), you can conclude that it will cost *at least* $600 to produce a quality e-book. I raided my very small retirement account to publish my six books, and I considered it a small business loan to myself. I now treat my novel-writing career as a business instead of a hobby and it has paid off for me.

How long does it take to earn back a $600–$1,000 investment? That depends on many things, including how many novels you have on the market. The more books you have, the more credibility you have, which is why I decided to do all mine back to back. Assuming you've written a terrific story and produced a quality product, the biggest factor is how much time you're willing to spend promoting. I spent at least two hours a day for six months, plus one exclusive two-week period during which I promoted eight hours a day (blogs, press releases, reader forums, etc.). I continue to spend at least an hour every day on promotional activities even when I'm writing a new novel. In between drafts, promoting is full-time work. For the record, I made my money back by the end of the year, and going forward is all profit.

It's your book and you've invested your money, you might as well invest your time too and make it pay off.

Why $.99 E-Books Don't Work for Me (7/11)

I've gone back and forth for months trying to decide whether to price my new release, *The Arranger*, at $.99 or $2.99…for the launch phase. The thinking is this: At 99 cents, I'll sell more copies, the book will go higher on the Amazon charts, and I'll get more exposure. But I won't make much money…unless it hits the top of the charts and stays there for a long time. But can I count on that?

Of course not. In July, I conducted an experiment and priced all my Jackson books at $.99. They got a little bump in sales, then quickly settled into a level slightly higher than where they'd been at $2.99, for example 25 books a day for one title compared to 15 at the lower price. The problem is the royalty. Amazon only pays a 35% royalty on books under $2.99, instead of 70%. So dropping a price from $2.99 to $.99 not only means charging a third of the price, it also means receiving half of the royalty.

Straight-up math: I have to sell six times as many books at the lower price to make exactly the same money. That's hard to pull off. There are so many authors and publishers now offering their books at $.99 that it's hard to gain much attention with that price, especially since my books have been on the market a while and already reached thousands of readers.

My experiment taught me this: I can't make a living selling my books at $.99. Yet, I have to make a living. I'm a full-time novelist now, and I don't want to go back to freelancing. If I were to start editing again, I would write less and disappoint my readers who are waiting for the next Jackson book.

So all my novels are now back to the higher price, and *The Arranger* will be released at $2.99. It's still a great bargain for readers. I may put certain books on sale for short periods of time, but I may not. Readers like consistency, and I'm sure they're as tired of the price fluctuations as I am.

Chapter 10: Nonfiction Articles
(Features published in *The Register Guard*, 09–10)

Surgeon With Heart

For most young women, planning for college is a matter of filling out paperwork. For Hoang Nguyen, a native of South Vietnam who's now a cardiothoracic surgeon, it meant putting her life on the line, crossing a treacherous ocean in a boat with a converted motorcycle engine, and braving unimaginable hardship.

As a 17-year-old in South Vietnam in 1981, Hoang (pronounced Whan) had no chance of higher education. Her father had worked for the U.S. military, so the communist government, which had recently taken over, would never allow her or anyone in her family to attend a university.

Hoang was determined to

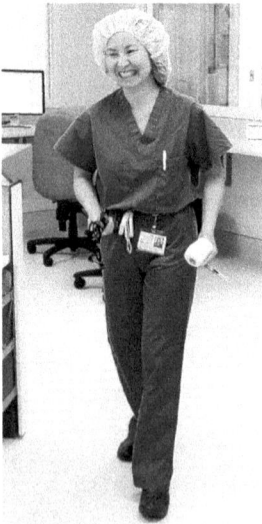

leave the country. "I always wanted to go to school," she says, "and everyone said the United States was the best place to get an education."

Hoang's parents learned of a boat planning an escape and helped recruit enough people to make it possible. In exchange, they earned places on the boat for Hoang and two of her siblings. Others who hoped to leave paid in gold—usually a significant sum in a country where paper currency had little value.

The boat was made of wood, barely seaworthy, and powered by a converted motorcycle engine. Still, 117 people boarded the craft while bullets flew over their heads. If they had been captured, prison or labor camp awaited them.

"At that time, I thought the worst thing that could happen was that I would die," say Hoang. "I was so naïve."

The boat was intended to hold 60 or 70 people, so with 117 on board, the conditions soon became unbearable. "I stayed out on the open end of the boat," Hoang says. "I got soaked from the rain, and my sister and I had to tie ourselves to the boat sometimes to not get washed overboard, but I couldn't go in the covered part. It was too horrible."

For seven days and six nights, they were at sea. Storms raged, the engine broke down once, and they ended up off course. "You feel so small out there," Hoang says, her beautiful face beginning to show the emotional toll of telling her story.

They finally arrived on the tiny island of Kota in the Philippines. Hoang spent the next two years in a series of refugee camps, living in tents she and her siblings made from what they could find in the surrounding jungle. Nearly 30 years later, it still makes her cry to remember some of the other young women in the camps who had been raped or forced into prostitution. "I was very lucky," she says.

Hoang was also very determined to get to the United States. If she had been willing to settle for Australia, she could have left the camps in six months. Entry to the U.S. was more difficult, and she endured repeated interrogations about her interest in coming to America.

Finally, at the age of 19, she arrived in Oklahoma, sponsored by a Baptist church. Hoang soon enrolled in community college and learned English as she went along. She started with science classes because "a formula is a formula in any language." While earning a five-year pharmacy degree, Hoang applied to medical school at the University of Oklahoma.

"I thought at first my English wasn't good enough for medical school, that's why I went to pharmacy school," she recalls. "But I wanted to be a doctor, so I applied anyway." It's easy to think the admissions board must have been impressed with all that Hoang had accomplished in a few short years in a new country with new a language.

Her accomplishments were just getting started. She went on to earn two medical board certificates, one in general surgery and one in thoracic surgery, and she's currently the only woman surgeon on staff at the Oregon Heart and Vascular Institute.

As a young altruistic doctor fresh out of medical school, Hoang applied to return to Vietnam, wanting to help people who had not had her good fortune. The Vietnamese government turned her down. "I got mad that I was not welcome even as a volunteer," she says. "So I've never been back."

Hoang practiced in New Mexico for years, then left when the hospital and physician group changed owners and became a for-profit organization. One of the appeals of the Sacred Heart position was its nonprofit status.

"I love taking care of people," Hoang says of her job. "I love to see them get better because of my help."

Have Pen, Will Travel (Creator of Stone Soup)

Jan Eliot learned a few things about herself last fall while traveling on back-to-back international excursions. First she discovered a love for tuk tuks, little three-wheeled taxis, and wrote her own ideal obituary: *Died in a tuk tuk in Thailand while on a humanitarian mission.*

While traveling in Algeria, she had a more serious self-discovery. "I realized I had started to allow myself to feel like I was getting a little bit old," Jan recalls. "And I thought, 'Damn, I'm not old. Look where I am. I'm in Algeria, and I'm by myself for a week. And there are checkpoints and people with machine guns everywhere.'"

Cultural ambassador: How did the Eugene creator of the *Stone Soup* comic strip end up in Algeria? She received an invitation from the U.S. Bureau of Educational and Cultural Affairs to attend an international gathering of cartoonists held in Algiers. The exhibition's hosts invited mostly cartoonists from French-speaking countries, but they also wanted a well-known American female political cartoonist, and they asked the U.S. Department of State to choose someone. Sensitive to diplomatic relations, the state department wanted to send a cartoonist who wrote a strip about a family, and they narrowed it down to Lynn Johnston (creator of *For Better or For Worse*) and Jan Eliot.

"Lynn was already committed to an exhibition in Montreal, so it came to me," Jan says. "And I said, 'Sure, I've never been to North Africa. I'll go in minute.'"At the exhibition, Jan met graphic artists from around the world and gave talks about how comic strips are created and syndicated, which is unique to the United States. She also participated on a panel and answered questions about censorship of the market-place vs. the legal censorship that cartoonists in Africa experience.

"I got bolder as I went along and talked about a lot of feminist principles too," Jan says. While she was there, she also visited an orphanage, a troubled-child center, and a women's shelter—accompanied by a bodyguard everywhere she went. The U.S. Embassy in Algeria had sent out notice to neighboring countries that an American cartoonist would be visiting, so Jan ended up making a side trip to Morocco, where she gave talks at four graphic arts schools in four days. She spoke with students in Casablanca, Rabat, Tangiers, and Tetouan.

"Some of the students I met looked as if they had come in their one change of clothes," she says. "But everybody had a USB stick, so they could put it in any computer that opened up and show their work." Many of the artists she met gave Jan samples of their work to bring home, and she cherishes the cocktail napkin on which a student drew her a caricature of himself.

House #52: Soon after unpacking from Algeria, Jan was back in the air. This time she flew to Thailand with Women Build, a subgroup of Habitat for Humanity, and spent a week laying bricks in the heat. She worked side-by-side with the Thai family who would occupy the completed home (House #52) one of 82 being built in Chiang Mai in honor of King Bhumibol Adulyadej's 82nd birthday. The home Jan helped to construct is small and simple by American standards, but a luxury for the receiving family.

"We're building houses for people who have been hauling water from rivers and sleeping under corrugated tin," she explains. "So to have a cement block house with a cement foundation and plumbing with running water is a huge step up."

In the evenings, the crew (which included Jet Li and Janet Huckabee) was free to have fun. "You could get on the bus and go to posh hotels and see a show or be exposed to the Thai culture in any way you wanted," Jan says. "Or jump in a tuk tuk and go see it for yourself." Jan's involvement with Women Build started seven years ago when the group contacted her to create an illustration for its Girls Build educational materials, featuring her young comic strip characters, Holly and Alex. Next Jan designed a T-shirt for Women Build that showed her adult characters, Val and Joan, holding building tools. "The whole goal of Women Build is to get more women involved," Jan says. "And to make sure they learn the skills and are not just doing the fetching."

Eventually Women Build sent Jan to worksites to pound nails for a day in hopes of using her well-known status to attract the media. Jan worked on a house in New Orleans as part of the Hurricane Katrina rebuild, one in Suffolk County, N.Y., and one in Silverton, OR. Next, came the invitation to fly to Thailand and join the Jimmy and Rosalynn Carter Foundation for a full week of construction.

International travel is not a new experience for the cartoonist. Her sister lives in Austria and her daughter is in Germany, so Jan travels overseas frequently. She's also visited Switzerland, Italy, Greece, France, Spain, Portugal, England, Scotland, the Czech Republic, the Netherlands, Turkey, Uganda, Kenya, Zanzibar, Canada and Mexico. Next up? Probably Australia. "I can't think of another reason to work than to be able to travel," Jan says. "I'm not happy unless I have a plane ticket in the drawer and something in the works."

Sergeant Kathy Flynn

As a student of English literature, Kathy Flynn never imagined she would one day carry a gun and conduct a traffic stop that would almost turn deadly. "When I was young, if anybody had told me I would be a police officer, I would have wondered what they were smoking," says Sergeant Kathy Flynn, who supervises the Eugene Police Department's violent crimes unit. It makes her laugh to think of it even now. Yet a series of decisions brought her to a career that occasionally puts her life on the line.

While still a patrol officer, Kathy stopped a driver at the request of another officer. After being pulled over, the driver became agitated and uncooperative. Kathy went back to her car to run a background check while the second officer tried to calm the detainee. When she looked up, the situation had escalated.

"The officer shouted, 'Show me your hands!' " Kathy recalls. "Then I saw the other officer had his gun out and was pointing it through the window. Then I saw the man leaning over and he was getting something. We both thought he was going for a gun. So I drew mine. The man came up and he had something in his hand."

Kathy ran for the vehicle, gun drawn. "Then he punched his hand out the window," Kathy says, gesturing with surprising force. "I had pressure on the trigger, but I didn't have a shot. And it's a good thing, because what the guy had in his hand was a tape recorder."

The incident took place on 13th and Kincaid with University of Oregon students everywhere, and Kathy couldn't risk injuring a bystander. The man was given a ticket and let go. Apparently there's no law against scaring the hell out of police officers.

Kathy's levelheadedness and decision-making skills have served her well in her 22 years with the Eugene Police Department. But it wasn't a career she had planned on. Fresh out of college with bachelor's degrees in English literature and sociology, she worked first as a horse trainer, then eventually as a banker in Ashland. On a whim and needing to shake up her life, Kathy moved to Eugene and applied for a job as a communications specialist.

"I thought, 'Well shoot, I can communicate,'" she says, laughing at her naiveté. "I had no idea what it was." The communications job actually entailed working as a 911 dispatcher. Kathy made it through the exhaustive screening process and worked as a dispatcher for two and a half years. Then one evening during a ride-along in a patrol car, an officer encouraged her to apply for a police position.

"Again, I thought, 'Why not?'" she says. It's unusual to start a career in law enforcement in your 30s, but Kathy has never let cultural expectations get in her way. Even as a child, she refused to accept that girls couldn't be crossing guards or sell TV guide subscriptions. "From the time I was little I didn't understand why people were telling me I couldn't do things because I was a girl." Now as a police sergeant, Kathy supervises a team of eight male detectives. She says gender is not currently an issue for her, but it wasn't always the case.

"That was a pretty crusty crowd back then," Kathy says, referring to her initial training with the violet crimes unit in 1988. "Violent crimes (units) tend to have people with strong personalities because of the nature of the work."

Kathy spent half her police career working patrol, much of it as a sergeant, and half in detective work. "I love both," she says. "They're both awesome." During her two decades in the department, Kathy has been assigned to traffic control, the university station, schools, and violent crimes. Her diverse experience has fostered understanding of, and rapport with, an entire network that includes child services, the district attorney's office, patrol and probation, sexual assault services, and others.

She believes that background helped her earn her current position, which she calls "the best job in the department." "It's very beneficial to have that bigger view of the community and understand the system in all its complexity," Kathy says.

It's Never Too Late for Humor

Patrice Dotson loves to try new things. Over the course of a long life, she's been a medical technician, a psychologist, a masseuse, an artist, and a marketing director. At the age of 77, she decided to add stand-up comic to the list. "I was bored," she says. "I had done just about everything I could think of to do. Life was getting dull, and I didn't have much to laugh about."

Then a friend invited Patrice to a Comedy Workout performance. There, she met Leigh Anne Jasheway, heard about her comedy writing class and thought, why not?

Putting pen to paper and writing comedy is the week-to-week expectation of the LCC-sponsored class, but the goal after eight weeks is to get up in front of a crowd and make them laugh. Not everyone has the courage to take that final step. Many who do are terrified. Patrice, on the other hand, boldly came on stage with shocking-pink spiked hair. She did the first half of her set about "the funny things that happen to you when you're and older person," then dazzled the crowed with her bit about "little penises." "I don't think there's anything funnier," she says, with her soft deadpan delivery.

She describes the performance experience as "a lot of fun" and "liberating." "I was able to present a part of myself that I usually don't show to the world," she says. "It's kind of like wearing a clown suit, like being someone other than who you're expected to be."

The experience was so much fun, Patrice plans to perform again this month at the Northwest Women's Comedy Festival, held at the Wildish Theater in Springfield on Nov. 21. With nine other comics on the roster, some of whom are professionals from other states, the event is sure to draw a much bigger crowd than Patrice's first performance.

But she's not intimidated. In fact, she's taking the class again so she'll be disciplined about writing new material. "This time my stuff is about Catholicism," she says, "such as 'things you probably shouldn't do in church.'"

Taking the class the first time proved to be more than just learning about the different types of comedy. It was a group of all women who bonded so well, they still meet once a month for dinner to catch up and talk about their new material.

"It was the best class and the best group of people," Patrice says. "I loved the class and how it made me feel."

Her ability to make people laugh may be in the genes. Her son in Seattle also worked as a stand-up comic for a while, and Patrice loves his sense of humor. Her favorite comic though is Ellen Degeneres. "She's bright and quick and never mean or foul," Patrice explains.

Patrice's goal as a comedian is to get on the "casino circuit." "I think my humor would suit that older crowd," she says. "But everyone really needs humor today. People are angry and afraid, and it's a gift to be able to make people laugh."

Author's current note: I took this class years earlier and have performed standup comedy several times in that club. ☺

Raising the Bar

It takes a special kind of person to be so committed to a goal that it factors into nearly every single life decision. Sarah Bertram is that kind of person. The 26-year-old champion weightlifter has her eye on making the 2012 Olympic team, and she won't let anything get in her way. Vacations are out of the question; they take too much time away from training. Even a two-day skiing excursion must be sacrificed because the potential for injury is too high. Staying out late and skipping meals after a workout are not options either, no matter what fun activity her friends have planned.

"It can be hard to have a flexible social life," she says, "but I love this sport. I love the challenge and the hard work." The challenge requires Sarah to train five days a week. For 90 minutes, she works the bar and its free weights, exerting her way through dozens of squats and lifts. Afterward, she powers through some pull-ups and ab work just for good measure.

Sarah makes a point to clarify that Olympic weightlifting and powerlifting are distinctive sports, each with their own bar, plates, techniques, and lifts. She also doesn't want her endeavor to be confused with bodybuilding, which is in another category that is "completely aesthetic."

Sarah's dream of making the Olympic team took a giant leap forward in 2009 when she won the U.S. national championship in her weight class (69 kg/152 pounds), making her the best "light heavyweight" lifter in the country. Her trip to the world championships in Korea in November 2009, where she placed 16th, brought her even closer.

"When you compete at this level, you get to point where you can't just muscle something anymore," she explains. "So it comes down to technique and mental focus and momentum. It's a lot more technical than people think."

A passion is born: Sarah's passion for the sport began in high school when she started weightlifting as a strength-training workout for her track-and-field pursuits. "Olympic weightlifting has good carryover functionally for any sport," she explains. "It builds explosiveness and speed and strength." The training paid off and as a high school senior, Sarah qualified for state competition in the javelin. She grew to love the challenging new sport and it soon became her athletic focus.

During her four years at the University of Oregon, where she earned a bachelor of fine arts degree, Sarah trained independently at Ironworks Gym in Creswell. Most colleges, including the UO, don't support Olympic weightlifting teams, so the athletes must join local gyms and clubs to train and compete. Sarah feels fortunate to have access to a gym with the right equipment and a skilled trainer.

Her coach, Tom Hirtz, who was once an Olympic competitor, has been with her at every training session for the past nine years. "When I met Sarah, she was a young, skinny girl who was not that strong," Hirtz recalls. "It's been a long, hard road for her, but she has the special determination that only a few have. She has a lot of guts, diligence, and a real strong work ethic. Now she's getting to the top of her game." After Sarah placed fourth in the national championships in 2008, Hirtz wrote on the board in the gym: "Sarah Bertram, 2009 National Champion, 69 kilograms."

The weightlifter saw that goal every day for a year. Then she went to the meet and made it happen. In 2010, she placed sixth in the national championships, bringing her a step closer to her Olympic-team goal. "This sport has made me confident and focused," she says. "And that carries over into every other area of my life as well."

Benefits of weightlifting: Sarah's belief in the benefits of weightlifting motivated her to join Coach Hirtz in his volunteer outreach to at-risk youths in the John Serbu detention center. Three days each week for the past six years, Sarah has volunteered her time and passed along her training to help troubled young people build confidence and self-discipline.

"Sarah is such an inspiration to these kids," Hirtz says. Although she won't always be a national competitor, Sarah believes Olympic weightlifting always will be part of her life. She also thinks more women would get involved in the sport if they understood it better. The misconception she would most like to correct is that "Olympic weightlifting will make you big."

"It takes a long time to get big," she explains. "And you can stop accelerating long before that happens. When I first started lifting, I lost weight and got more toned." As a fine arts graduate, Sarah's second love is ceramics and she looks forward to having more time for her art someday. But she has no regrets about her choices or focus, adding, "If I look ahead ten years from now, I know I'll be happy that I did this while I was young and tried to be the best I could be."

Sugar and Spice Sisters

Most people experience a point in their lives when circumstances come together to alter the course of the future. For sisters Cheryl and Catherine Reinhart, that moment occurred soon after college when they had both broken up with boyfriends and wanted a change in their lives. Cheryl, three years older, called Catherine and said, "We're going out West." And Catherine said, "Let's go."

That was the turning point that brought them to Eugene, where the sisters later started their own successful bakery called Sweet Life Patisserie. But after spending only an hour with the women, it's easy to see that the sisters' bond is so tight that if it had not been a trip out West in an old VW van, some other set of circumstances would have drawn them together in a way that intertwined their lives. Except for their college years—Cheryl at Cornell in New York and Catherine at Boston University—the sisters have always lived in the same house or neighborhood. "We're right around the corner from each other," Cheryl says, "and we like it that way."

Growing up together: After their parents divorced—at the time Cheryl was eight and Catherine was five—they moved from the Bay Area in California to Thornville, Ohio, with their mother, Patricia Reinhart. It was in that setting the siblings began to bond. "We were in a rural area, so we spent most of our free time at home," Cheryl recalls. "We did 4H, and we raised animals, and we both were in the drama club at school."

Catherine also spent ample time in the kitchen, making cookies and candy and decorating each piece individually. "I love sugar," she says with a laugh. "Baking was a way to have the sugar."

"They made my life easier," their mother, Patricia, comments. "I told them I needed their help, and they understood that. They had a lot of responsibilities."

Still, they had issues like any other siblings. "Cheryl was the older sister who would be mean to me sometimes," Catherine recalls. "And I was the poor little 'me' sister. It was just something we had to go through."

Cheryl remembers it a little differently. Turning to her sister, she says, "You were really close to Mom, and I was the antagonist, the outsider. It was just the three of us, so it was a weird dynamic."

Young adults on the move: Under those aprons, the Reinhart sisters are hardy women who have challenged themselves repeatedly. They both spent time in Africa in their early 20s, and after a few months of traveling the West Coast, at Cheryl's urging, they took jobs on a fishing boat in Alaska.

"We worked 12 hours a day, every day, for four months, and sometimes we worked round the clock," Cheryl recalls. "The captain told us he didn't think we would last out our four-month contract. He didn't know we had a hard-core working class mom who had taught us to work hard."

Catherine fills in the details: "We started with four cooks, but two of them left, so it was just the two of us, serving a crew of 90. We were cooking and mopping and doing dishes. It was crazy, but we made it." The reward for their tenacity was a paid flight back to Seattle and $9,000 in savings for each of them.

Catherine saw the money as an opportunity to buy property, something their mother had drilled into them as a better option than renting. Cheryl still wanted to travel. While Catherine went back to Ohio to get the rest of their belongings, Cheryl spent a month in Guatemala.

Settling down. They met back in Eugene and bought a house in the Whiteaker neighborhood. Like many other East Coasters who end up here, they had come through Eugene during their Pacific travels and fell in love with the town. Their dream was eventually to buy a farm and live the country life. The boat-cook job was at the top of their résumés, so they found work in local restaurants. Looking back, the sisters make jokes about their "nice liberal arts degrees" and how "college enriched our minds."

They often worked in the same restaurant or bakery, but discovered that "bosses tried to pit us against each other." Other employers were "angry or unhappy" or too rigid in their approach to creating desserts. "I was bursting with creative energy and I felt squelched," Catherine says. "I realized it was always going to be that way working for someone else." One night while sitting on the back porch, they decided to start their own business. "We realized it wasn't rocket science," Cheryl says. "We thought if they could do it, we could do it." So they converted their garage into a licensed bakery and started making wedding cakes.

Becoming partners. Sweet Life Patisserie began simply enough, but it quickly became successful. Learning to operate a business wasn't that challenging for the bright women.

"We picked up what we needed along the way," Cheryl says. "We studied, we talked things out, and we applied logic." Learning to work together full time was more challenging. "Cheryl can say something to me, and because she's my sister, it's like pushing this button right here," Catherine says, pointing to her torso. "Someone else could say exactly the same thing, and it wouldn't bother me. A mountain of history comes with the phrase." After they expanded their business to include the retail store, the sisters sought counseling to make their relationship better. Cheryl says, "It has been really good for us to be adults who work together. Because our relationship is completely different now. We balance each other."

Their personalities are distinct, yet hard to characterize. Cheryl, who now has three children, is more analytical and prefers to move more slowly on a decision. Yet she's the one with the adventurous spirit who went to Africa with the Peace Corps, spent a month in Guatemala, and wanted to work on the fishing boat in Alaska. Catherine is more creative and impulsive, yet she pushed to purchase real estate, start the business, then expand it. She also would rather be "Auntie" than a mother.

"I gave them permission to be anything they wanted," Patricia says. She was surprised at first that her daughters had chosen to work in restaurants, then start their own. But she's not surprised they've spent so much time with each other. "When they were kids, we ate all our meals together, we gardened together, we did everything together. It was all about family."

The Whiners

They've been kicked to the back of restaurants for having too much fun. They go bowling in goofy costumes and give each other bizarre Christmas gifts just for kicks. Women Humorously Irreverent about Nearly Everything, aka the Whiners, have been hanging out together for 26 years—and the laughter is what keeps them going.

After decades of lunches, birthdays, and themed parties, their memories are fuzzy, and sometimes they have to get out the photographs to be certain who dressed in the cheerleader outfit or who brought the crucifix-shaped meatloaf. But looking back is part of the fun. "We're the keepers of each other's history," says Judith Manning, summing up how everyone feels.

The group first got together in 1983 when most of the women worked for the Springfield Utility Board. They would go out for birthday lunches at El Kiosco, where the staff quickly learned to move them to the back room. The lunches expanded to happy hours, and eventually the women started gathering for potlucks at members' homes where no one could shush them or toss them out. They discovered a mutual love of movies, which led to Academy Awards nights, jazzed up by dressing in Oscar-worthy gowns or as a favorite movie star.

Once the costumes got started, there was no holding back. The group quickly adopted any opportunity to wear hats, togas, or feather boas. After a few wild Academy Awards evenings, more theme parties followed. Bowling for Identities, in which the women bowled in costumes of their choice, led Kris Garrick to create her "Stinky" character, a nerd complete with high-waisted pants, taped-together glasses, and a funny voice. "This group has made me a little more fearless in all ways," Kris says. "Once you go beyond worrying about what people are going to think, you can just go nuts and not care."

Kate Tryhorn once hosted an English tea party, where they all dressed "in little suits and gloves." The prim and properness lasted all of five minutes before devolving into the usual raucous roar. "They've been there for everything," Kate says in describing what the Whiners have meant to her. "They are the most constant thing in my life. We all change, but the group doesn't change."

The Whiners have held a swimming party, a séance, and once played Pin the Tail on a nude male model poster, only they weren't aiming for the tail. Putting their own spin on games is a favorite activity. They've played a twisted version of Truth or Dare called Well I Never, which quickly became a contest to shock each other. "Oh my God," Jo Dahlin says. "It was crazy." At a party hosted by Cynthia Spencer, the women played their own version of Fictionary. They faked the words, made up their own definitions, and "came unglued." The phrase "Rogation Days" came up. No one remembers how they defined it, but they all remember spitting out their drinks in laughter. A new standard for funny was set.

"These women are the connection to the best and the worst times in my life," Cynthia says. "When I was in a horrible job, they made it manageable. I've come and gone from the group a few times because I moved, but when I come back, it's like I never left." The friends have had their serious moments. Early on, they held a baby shower for Pauline Clark, and every Whiner put something into a time capsule for Pauline's daughter to open when she turned 16. The group was all there a decade and a half later when Kelsey opened the sealed capsule. "These people are loyal and supportive," Pauline says, her voice filled with emotion. "The year my mother died, Mary Ann took me to Utah to the Sundance Film Festival. She really took care of me."

Supporting each other through the tears is as much a Whiner trait as making each other laugh. They feel fortunate they've had many more opportunities to laugh. Mary Ann Rhodes is famous for her Christmas parties, which in Whiner world are the most irreverent of all. Good Gifts/Bad Gifts is a popular theme, with bad gifts being the most fun. One year, Jo gift-wrapped a toilet seat with a picture of Richard Nixon on the lid. Peggy Potter once gave a crocheted candleholder that generated more than its share of lewd comments. When Peggy (the ninth member) moved to Montana, the group held a séance in honor of her parting. Judith, dressed in her finest gypsy clothes, brought a crystal ball and conjured up people from Peggy's life. Whiners dressed in character, giving a spiel. Nancy Gentry appeared as Peggy the high-school cheerleader, Kate offered guidance as Peggy's mother, and Kris came as a gossipy janitor from their workplace.

Over the years, the Whiners have been there for each other's weddings and divorces, births and deaths, cancer treatments, and career changes. When Nancy earned her psychology degree and left her job at SUB, they hosted a special last-day-of-work party. Nancy had once mentioned a desire to leave work at noon and never come back. Her friends made it happen in glorious Whiner style. They swooped her up in a champagne-filled limo with everyone dressed for an evening on the town, topped by glitter-covered sombreros made by Kate. They had a formal portrait taken, lunched at Mount Pisgah, and lounged at the Valley River Inn. Throughout the afternoon, they serenaded Nancy with songs written for the occasion.

"We'll all be talking at once, then someone will break into a song or a dance," Nancy says. "There are no inhibitions here. These are the most creative, intelligent and vibrant women I know." Twenty-six years ago, the Whiners saw each other as "kindred spirits," and that feeling hasn't changed. "It's family," Kris says, describing her bond to the group. "It's better than family," Jo adds, laughing. "These people are fun."

Family With Flair

As a little girl, Donna Marisa Bontrager wanted to dance, but her parents thought she should play the piano instead. So her ballet career didn't begin until she was 18, practically unheard of among professional dancers. Later, when her own daughters, Hannah and Ashley, were young, she was determined they would have the opportunity she'd been denied.

Today, the three Bontrager women—mom and daughters—run their own ballet academy and chamber company, Ballet Fantastique, producing critically acclaimed performances and attracting talented cast members from around the country.

Born to dance: Although she didn't take her first dance class until she was a student at the University of Oregon, Donna quickly realized it was meant to be. "I fell in love with ballet. I just knew that was what I was supposed to do. It was what was in my heart," she says. Her natural talent made up for lost time, and Donna went on to dance with several professional ballet companies in New York state. In time, she realized that ballet pedagogy, or teaching the movement of the dance, was her strength—especially combined with her knowledge of design and art. Eventually Donna moved with her young daughters back to Eugene, where it all started for her.

"Before we were born, she knew she wanted us to be dancers," says Hannah, the older offspring, who is now a driving force of Ballet Fantastique. "But I don't feel like she's living vicariously through us. She was never one of those stage moms who follow their kids around. She just wanted us to have this beautiful art form as part of our lives."

Ashley, coming along behind, felt a little more pressure. "Hannah was born to this, but I went through a few stages of not wanting to dance," she admits with a laugh. "In high school, I was not that excited about it because it took so much of my time. But I'm finally to the point where I'm thankful that I have something that I'm really good at. It's nice to have people admire what I do." There is much to admire about the Bontrager women. In addition to being professional ballerinas, choreographers, and directors of a nonprofit enterprise, all three women have a four-year college degree from the UO.

Donna's background is in architecture, Hannah has a bachelor's in English, and Ashley recently graduated from the university's journalism school. But ballet is their passion, and performance is in their blood.

Starting the academy. When the girls were still in high school, the family opened a dance school in a high-ceiling studio in the heart of downtown Eugene. With help from friends, they laid the sprung dance floor, hung out their shingle, and started taking in students.

"We would go door to door, asking people if they were interested in ballet classes," Donna says. "My dream was to have this kind of school." By that she means the Vaganova training method, a Russian style of ballet that requires dancers to understand intellectually the concepts they're learning. She also keeps the classes small so every student gets personal attention.

While earning their high school and college educations and working at the academy, Ashley and Hannah also continued to train with various teachers and dance companies. As their skills became more advanced, the sisters felt compelled to perform at a professional level. It was no longer enough to choreograph performances for their students. The idea of starting their own chamber company to create unique worldclass performances began to blossom.

To make it happen, the women learned to be much more than dancers. They had to collaborate with musicians, create and distribute posters, write press releases, solicit donations, and recruit dancers, interns, and volunteers. At first, they did most of the organizing themselves, with Hannah taking the lead on public relations and Donna overseeing the artistic direction, including making costumes. Ashley was the stabilizing presence who filled in where needed and kept them all grounded. The results: critically acclaimed performances year after year.

The women are quick to express gratitude for the volunteers and business sponsors who have helped them over the years. To give back to the community that has generously supported them, Ballet Fantastique holds fundraisers and offers scholarships to young dancers who otherwise could not afford the classes. "We believe no talented dancer should be denied the opportunity to train," Hannah says.

Embracing fate: Despite all the time and effort they pumped into the company during the past nine years, until recently the daughters didn't see Ballet Fantastique as their future. "I always entertained the idea of becoming a news anchor," Ashley says, "but now I'm starting to think I want to get certified in Pilates and fitness. It takes up so much of my life already, it would coincide a lot better for me, and I would still get to spend time with my family."

Hannah thought she would be an English teacher or possibly a graphic designer. Then Ballet Fantastique started "to really take off" and she realized that the family business is where her heart is. "Part of it was going to Washington, D.C. and dancing with a ballet company there and realizing that what we do here is just as unique and special," Hannah explains. "I realized I didn't have to go anywhere else to be successful."

For her own future, Donna sees herself continuing to "design dancers" in the academy and increasing the professional level of the chamber company's performances. For her daughters, though, she simply says, "What's most important is that they are happy and fulfilled in their lives."

Friends Forever

Some high-school friendships last a day; others, a lifetime. Enduring friendships often are built on a special bond, and sometimes they are the result of shared circumstances and proximity. In the case of two sets of best friends, who met up last month at their 40th high-school reunion, it's a combination of all that and more. Working on the reunion committee each decade since they graduated from Sheldon High School in 1969 brought these women together again and again—and reinforced the connections they first developed as middle schoolers.

Connie and Carol: Connie Peoples Hollingsworth and Carol Minihan Bartram met in a locker room at Monroe Junior High. Neither felt much like an athlete, and that shared insecurity formed an instant bond. "I would always say, 'Wait for me,'" recalls Carol. "And she would stay back. So we became friends."

Their friendship solidified in high school through a shared interest in drama and pep club. They spent time with each other's families, often traveling together, and even were hospital volunteers—known as candy stripers then—at the same time. "Carol's nickname in high school was Den Mother because she's Mother Earth and took care of everybody," Connie banters. Carol went on to pursue a career in healthcare administration, and Connie became a legal secretary, then a Bethel high-school secretary. Except for a brief time when Carol went to college in Corvallis, both women have lived in Eugene, making it easy to stay in touch. They have been there for each other at all the important life moments: weddings, births, and deaths.

"We've been through the wonderful joys of falling in love and having babies," says Carol. "And we've been through the terrible deaths of our parents. There are times I don't know what I would have done if I hadn't had her. She knows my heart deeper than anyone." Connie describes her friendship with Carol in almost identical terms. "It's the kind of friendship that even if we don't talk for a month, after the first five minutes, we know exactly where the other is at. This relationship has given me a sense of security, a sense of knowing who I am and where I've come from. I can go to her for anything." Because they have lived in Eugene all along, both women have been active members of the reunion committee. At each 10-year interval, they work passionately to plan the events and contact other old friends.

Nancy and Margie: Nancy Rissberger Kinnard and Margie Speer Watson met at Cal Young Junior High on the first day of school in 1965. They both remember it clearly. "I felt so out of place. I was like the little surfer girl in the land of raincoats and umbrellas," says Margie, who had just moved to Eugene from Southern

California. "Nancy was on the way to the office that day and she said 'hi' to me. I looked up and she had red hair and freckles. I'd never seen anyone like her before." Nancy recalls, "I walked in and there she was, this pretty little blond-haired California girl. I was new to the public schools, and she was new, so we were both nervous little girls. And it was great; we just became friends."

During their high-school years, the friends shared catechism, sports, and a love of music. "She had a small family, and I liked going to her house because it was always quiet," Nancy says. "And I'm one of nine kids, so she liked coming to my house because it was always chaotic." They each had other friends for periods of time, but they always met back up. "In high school, we traded boyfriends left and right," Margie says. In fact, Margie eventually married a guy Nancy had dated "for a day." After high school, Margie and her husband moved away from Eugene, and the two women drifted apart for a while. Later, when Margie, an accountant, was visiting her family in Eugene, she learned that Nancy had a little baby girl. "I had to go see her," Margie says. Out of the blue, Margie knocked on Nancy's door, and it was as if they had never been out of touch.

"I know that Margie is always going to be there," says Nancy, who works in banking. "I can just pick up the phone and call. The deep bond we have is really important to me." Describing their friendship, Margie says, "It has given me a link to the past. And we get together in the present. And we'll go forward together.

Nancy has the same stories that I remember. Nobody else knows that stuff about me."

The reunion committee. For their 10th, 20th, 30th and 40th reunions, Sheldon's Class of '69 reunion organizers met once a week at Valley River Inn for months to plan the events. Known as the " email queen," Margie spent countless hours tracking down classmates online. The women's efforts brought about 150 people to the 40th reunion, including 19 teachers and a man from Holland who had been a high-school exchange student in their class. Over the years the reunion committee's work reinforced the relationships of these four women. In a symbiotic way, their own lifelong friendships made them passionate advocates for the reunions—which helped their other classmates revisit special memories and re-embrace special friends.

Mother–Daughter Rowing Team

The first time Sally Keller entered a rowing competition in 1969, the regatta was sponsored by MIT's male crew team. The one race between women was considered a comedy event for entertainment. Only nobody told that to Sally and her team, at least until after they gave it their all and beat the other two boats by a wide margin. When Sally's team went looking for their prize, the sponsors informed them there was none. It was then she learned the men had not expected her crew to take the event seriously—or even finish the course.

Much has changed in women's sports since then. When Sally talks about her daughter, Kinsey Keller, also a competitive rower, the first thing she mentions is how times have changed. "When Kinsey went to college, she was able to join a full-fledged rowing program with intercollegiate competition," Sally says. Thirty years earlier, Sally had to form her own team, arrange her own competition, and borrow a boat from the men's club. Despite those cultural differences, the mother and daughter share a love for rowing that extends beyond membership in a club or the thrill of a race. "It's about grace and power, strength and balance," Sally says. "It uses every muscle in your body, and you have to constantly be aware of where your body is in space."

"It takes a strong personality," Kinsey adds, describing what she loves about rowing. "You get thrown into situations that are unexpected and demanding. It will toughen you up if you stick with it." It's also about the competition. Kinsey freely admits she loves to be first across the finish line. Sally—who rows year-round and often by herself in weather that might inspire others to curl up by a fire—would be out on the lake even if she never got to race. Yet Kinsey claims she gets her drive from her mother: "She's competitive, whether she admits it or not."

Living in different locations, the mother and daughter have not spent much time together in a boat. But the one time they raced as a team, they placed second in the national event and had great "fun!" "It was a thrown-together thing," Kinsey says. "So it was great knowing my mother had the experience to row well and that we could compete even though we hadn't practiced together." What Sally recalls is that, after the race, officials offered water to her daughter but not her. "She looked worse than I did," Sally says with a laugh.

The Kellers are both married to men who row, and as a family, they vacation together every year. These aren't "lie on the beach" holidays—they hike, crosscounty ski, or dream up some other athletic adventure. Kinsey's sister, Adrienne, doesn't row, but she bikes and hikes and keeps up with the rest of the family. A gymnast until high school, Kinsey almost didn't taking up rowing—just to buck the family trend. "They encouraged me, but because my parents did it, I was hesitant. I tried it anyway and got hooked." Their shared passion for rowing gives them another way to be involved in each other's lives.

As a graduate student, Kinsey doesn't have time to keep in shape for races, so she coaches instead. She and her mother often attend the same regattas, including the one pictured here at Dexter Lake in early April. Recruiting other women is another shared focus. They both describe rowing as a sport you can enter at any time in your life with no experience and be successful at it. "Some women have never done anything athletic in their life until they try this," Sally says. "Then they're like, 'Wow!' And they get into the best shape of their life at 50 or 60." This Saturday is National Learn to Row

Day, and Sally and Kinsey will be out at Dexter Lake showing others the sport they love.

Caring for All Creatures

A love of animals can bring together people of all walks of life. This is the heartfelt message Lyn Gilman-Garrick takes with her after 10 years of volunteer work with Pro-Bone-O, an organization that offers free pet care to homeless people. The idea was born nearly 12 ago years when Lyn managed Pacifica Veterinary Services for Dr. Doreen Hock and the two women became aware of the homeless community's need for pet care.

"A lot of transients would come in off the street with their dogs, asking for help," Lyn says. "They would often say, 'I don't have any money, but I'm willing to wash windows or sweep.' It was really obvious how much these people loved their animals but were absolutely unable to afford any care for them." For a year, Lyn and Doreen brainstormed ideas and recruited volunteers for the project, then called HALO (Helping Animals Living Outdoors).

With a law degree in her background and management experience, Lyn was the organizer who pulled together all the details to make it work. In 1998, the first clinic opened at the Catholic Community Services building on Seventh Avenue in Eugene. A few years later, the clinic moved to St. Vincent de Paul's service station on Highway 99.

For 11 years now, "like clock-work" the clinic has taken care of pets in the homeless community on the second and fourth Sunday of each month. During that decade, Lyn gave 10 to 20 hours a week to the cause, serving as founder, board member, secretary/treasurer, historian, office manager, and chief budget officer. Most of her time was spent recruiting veterinarians to staff the clinics.

Now nearly 25 vets are involved, about 30 nonmedical volunteers participate, and a collaboration with Oregon State University sends about 50 veterinary students each year to work with Pro-Bone-O. During her volunteer stint with the nonprofit, Lyn continued to manage Pacifica Veterinary Service and Healthy Pet, a holistic pet supply store. Her commitment went beyond simply giving her time. She and her husband, Paul, also offered a space in their home as Pro-Bone-O's office, which mostly serves as a place to store the donated supplies—vaccinations, flea collars, worm pills, and more.

"Every other Sunday we would schlep the supplies from the office out to St. Vincent DePaul's where the clinics were held," Lyn says. She is quick to point out that she is only one of dozens of dedicated volunteers who kept the clinic running, yet Vicki Bockes, a Pro-Bone-O board member, says, "I am convinced that without Lyn's persistence and perseverance, Pro-Bone-O would have disbanded at some point because it was too difficult, too daunting, too overwhelming, with too few resources."

Lyn recently retired from her manager job and her Pro-Bone-O work to take a cross-country bicycle trip from San Diego to Florida. "I'm looking forward to finding out what other passions I have," she says. One of those passions is the development of the Community Veterinary Center. Pro-Bone-O is collaborating with that new group and St. Vincent de Paul to establish a brick-and-mortar clinic that will serve not only the homeless, but all low-income pet owners, and will be open Monday through Friday. "It's very exciting to see that it's coming to fruition," Lyn says.

In addition to her current work with CVC, Lyn also volunteers with Cascade Hospice Service. She attributes her public service commitment to her involvement with Girl Scouts in high school. "As a Girl Scout, you're expected to be service-oriented and to do something worthwhile. You learn there's a bigger world out there and you should be a part of it." Lyn says that volunteer work with Pro-Bone-O can change people's perspective in how they view the homeless. "People say [about the homeless]: 'They can't even afford food; how can they afford an animal? What are they thinking?'" Lynn says, her voice catching with emotion. "If they saw the amount of comfort and security animals bring to homeless people, I don't think they would say that anymore."

Mid-Life Challenge

When Lori Rude was facing the double midlife whammy of the empty nest plus a looming 50th birthday, she knew she needed a new focus to get her through. She'd always been fit, with regular aerobic and weight-lifting sessions at the gym, but she decided to challenge herself with some serious cycling.

"Our youngest daughter was going off to college, and we, actually I, decided that my husband and I needed something more to fill up our time," she says. "He wasn't too keen on the whole biking thing at first, but he's athletic so he went along."

Switching gears: Up to that point, she and Scott were casual cyclists who went out occasionally on their mountain bikes for a "Sunday stroll." To test the waters, Lori signed them up for a 45-mile ride sponsored by Eola Hills Winery.

"We showed up in our regular clothes and tennis shoes," she recalls. "And I looked around at everyone else and realized I was a little bit out of my league. But we decided we could do it, and we did." They had a great time, and Lori began to wonder "what the possibilities were on a real road bike with the right equipment."

In other words, she was hooked.

They bought new bikes and started riding a lot more. Lori was looking at her 50th birthday coming up the next summer and thinking, "It would be a neat goal to do a long ride."

Then she heard about Cycle Oregon. "I went on the website and got really excited looking at all the neat things they do on the ride."

Giving herself a year or more to train, she set a goal of riding with Cycle Oregon in 2009 with a secondary goal of "not finishing last." She and her husband started doing 30-mile rides on Wednesdays with another couple and on Sundays with just the two of them. They kept it up until it was too dark and wet to ride over the winter, then resumed in early spring, putting in more than a 1,000 miles in a 12-month period.

When asked what was hardest about the training, Lori laughs and says, "Clip-on shoes." Then she adds, "And keeping up the stamina. Going like crazy and pedaling as hard as I can for two hours straight. It was hard."

Reaching the summit: After a year of training, it was finally time to test her endurance and tenacity. On a sunny Saturday in mid-September, Lori and Scott loaded their bikes and gear—one 50-pound bag each—and headed for Medford for the start of the 2009 Cycle Oregon ride.

Not surprising, the first day was the hardest. "After spending all morning doing switch-backs up to the Siskiyou summit," she recalls, "we got into a valley with a slight uphill and a 30-mile-an-hour headwind. That was tough. Everyone thought it was a tough day."

Day two, coming down the mountain was her favorite. "We were following the Klamath River through the canyon, and it was simply gorgeous and spectacular. The scenery for the whole trip was stunning."

Along the way, the 2,000 cyclists traveled through small towns such as Selma, Oregon and Happy Camp, California. Lori says their reception was one of the best things about the trip. "The way these small communities welcomed us, it was like we were rock stars," she comments. "They lined the streets and cheered, and you could tell this was the biggest thing to come to their town in a long time. It was great to meet the local people and see all the preparation they'd done."

The ride organizers also made sure the cyclists were entertained every evening with live music and various other events such as a bike mechanic rodeo. The trip was not without scary moments. One cyclist had a heart attack and was revived by the group medics, and another cyclist crashed and had to be airlifted to a hospital.

For Lori, the event was a triumph. After a week in the saddle for six or seven hours a day and 388 miles through the mountains, she reached her goal of finishing the ride—and not placing last. In fact, she was right in the middle of the pack.

"It was a hard ride and very challenging, and I loved every minute of it," she says. "We just may do it again next year."

Author's current note: Thanks for reading my book. If you enjoyed it, please leave a review or rating online. You can find out more about my novels at ljsellers.com. —L.J.

L.J. Sellers is an award-winning journalist and the author of the highly praised Detective Jackson mystery/suspense series:

  Secrets to Die For
  Thrilled to Death
  Passions of the Dead
  Dying for Justice
  Liars, Cheaters, & Thieves

She also has four standalone thrillers:

  The Sex Club
  The Baby Thief
  The Gantlet Assassin
  The Suicide Effect

When not plotting murders, L.J. enjoys performing standup comedy, cycling, social networking, and attending mystery conferences. She's also been known to jump out of airplanes.

Visist her website at: ljsellers.com

www.ingramcontent.com/pod-product-compliance
Lightning Source LLC
Chambersburg PA
CBHW060919040426
42445CB00011B/696